WACKY
Money

EVERT GONZÁLEZ

© Wacky 2024

All rights reserved. No part of this book may be reproduced, stored in a retrieval system, or transmitted, in any form or by any means, electronic, mechanical, photocopying, recording, or otherwise, without the prior written permission of the copyright holder.

This book is sold subject to the condition that it shall not, by way of trade or otherwise, be lent, resold, hired out, or otherwise circulated without the author's prior consent in any form of binding or cover other than that in which it is published and without a similar condition, including this condition, being imposed on the subsequent purchaser.

ISBN: 9798324316976
Imprint: Independently published

Inscription

To the curious minds and adventurous spirits,
Welcome to the whimsical world of 'Wacky Money'! Within these pages, you'll embark on a delightful journey through the quirky and unconventional side of finance. Prepare to be entertained, enlightened, and perhaps even a little bewildered as we explore the fascinating intersection of money and madness.

May this book inspire you to embrace the unexpected, challenge conventional wisdom, and approach the world of finance with a fresh perspective. Here's to unlocking the secrets of wacky money and discovering the joy in financial absurdity!

With warm regards,

About the Book

"Wacky Money" is not just a language learning book; it's a unique bridge between linguistic proficiency and financial literacy. In this comprehensive guide, language learners are immersed in captivating stories and real-life financial situations, equipping them with the language skills necessary to navigate the complex world of finance with confidence.

Delve into engaging narratives that take you beyond traditional language exercises, providing a context-rich environment for mastering the nuances of English. Each story is carefully crafted to balance linguistic development with a genuine understanding of financial expressions, creating an immersive and enjoyable learning experience.

Why Learn English Through Finance? Understanding and using English in financial contexts is a practical and valuable skill. Here's why "Wacky Money" encourages learners to explore language through the lens of finance:

Real-world Relevance: Finance is a universal language and integrating it into language learning adds immediate real-world relevance. From daily transactions to investment discussions, learners acquire language skills applicable in various situations.

Career Advancement: Proficiency in financial English enhances career prospects. Whether working in business, finance, or related fields, effective communication in financial contexts is a key asset.

Global Communication: As English continues to be the international language of business, learning financial English ensures learners can communicate effectively on a global scale, fostering cross-cultural connections.

Practical Language Use: The book goes beyond theory, providing practical language use in authentic financial scenarios. Learners not only understand words but also gain the ability to use them confidently.

Cultural Understanding: Finance often reflects cultural nuances and societal trends. Learning English through finance provides insights into cultural perspectives on money matters.

Overview of Topics: "Wacky Money" covers a wide range of topics, gradually progressing in difficulty to accommodate learners of all levels. The topics include:

Banking Basics: Opening accounts, payment systems, and discussing transactions.

Everyday Finances: Paying bills, budgeting, and conversations about saving and spending money.

Financial Situations: *Currency exchange, winning the lottery, and navigating business bookkeeping.*

Financial Challenges: *Handling hotel bills, supermarket checkouts, and addressing mistakes.*

Negotiating and Investing: *Bargaining with sellers, discussing get-rich-quick schemes, and understanding interest rates.*

Personal Finance: *Asking for raises, talking about wealth, and managing taxes.*

Special Money Situations: *Using ATMs, understanding rich and poor dynamics, and overcoming financial setbacks.*

Advanced Topics: *Buying luxury items, discussing foreign currency exchange rates, and exploring unique money situations.*

This book is designed to cater to learners at different proficiency levels, providing a well-rounded and progressively challenging learning experience. Whether you're a beginner or an advanced learner, "Wacky Money" offers a unique approach to language acquisition through the captivating world of finance.

Inscription 3
About the Book 4
   Opening a Bank Account 10
   Understanding Different Payment Systems 13
   Paying Bills 17
   Talking About Financial Goals 21
   Changing Money 24
   Winning the Lottery 27
   Business Bookkeeping 30
   Get-Rich-Quick Schemes 34
   A Mistake in the Hotel Bill 38
   The Supermarket Checkout 41
   Asking for a Raise 45
   Understanding Interest Rates 48
   Talking About Wealth 52
   Filing Taxes 56
   Talking About Prices 59
   Using an ATM 62
   Being Rich and Poor 65
   Recovering After a Setback 69

Buying a Luxury Car 73
Exchanging Rates 76
Collecting Debt 79
Giving Correct Change 82
Spending Money 85
Different Payment Systems 88
Living on Low Wages 91
Ending Excessive Spending 94
Having Bad Credit 97
Talking to a Bank Teller 101
Bargaining with the Store Owner 104
Getting Your Pocket Picked 107
Dealing With Debt 111
Negotiating Price 115
Paycheck Deductions 118
Reselling Products for Profit 121
Investing Your Money 125
Having Cash Flow Problems 129
Checking Accounts and Writing Checks 133
Wiring Money to Another Country 137
Reducing Household Expenses 141
Types of Bank Accounts 144
Marrying a Gold Digger 147

Using Coupons and Rebates 151

Being in Debt 155

Accepting Credit Cards as a Payment Option .158

Problem with a Restaurant Check 161

A Mistake in a Hotel Bill 164

Making a Bet 167

Black Friday 169

File Tax Return 172

Tax Refund 175

Budgeting for a Family 178

Living Paycheck to Paycheck 181

Investing in Stocks and Bonds 184

Saving for Retirement 187

Buying vs. Renting a Home 190

Starting a Side Hustle 193

Paying Off Student Loans 196

Teaching Kids About Money 198

Living on a Tight Budget 201

Using Credit Wisely 204

The Cost of Higher Education 207

The Impact of Inflation 210

Financing a Vacation 213

Dealing with Unexpected Expenses 216

Choosing the Right Insurance 219
Planning a Wedding on a Budget 222
The Benefits of Cashback and Rewards Credit Cards 225
Understanding Cryptocurrency 229
Borrowing Money from Friends or Family 232
Making Big Purchases: Cash or Credit 235
The Pros and Cons of Payday Loans 238
Sharing Expenses with Roommates 241
Charitable Giving on a Budget 244
Money Habits in Different Cultures 247
About the author 250
Conclusion 251
Acknowledgments and Resources 253

Opening a Bank Account

Lily: Hey, Mark! How's it going?

Mark: Oh, hey, Lily! I'm doing well. Just been trying to **figure out** some things with my bank. Actually, I'm thinking of **opening up** a new account.

Lily: That's exciting! I've been meaning to do that too. Are you switching banks or just **starting fresh** with a new type of account?

Mark: I'm actually switching banks. I've been with my current bank for years, but I've realized I need something with fewer fees and more online options. I've been putting it off for a while, but it's time to **take care of** it.

Lily: Smart move! So, have you already **looked into** any options?

Mark: Yeah, I did a little research. I found a few banks that **offer up** pretty good deals, but I'm still not sure which one to choose. I think I'll **stop by** a few branches this weekend and ask about their services in person.

Lily: That sounds like a good plan. You should definitely **check out** the fees, because that can make a huge difference. Oh, and when you're there, make sure you **bring along** some identification, like your ID or passport. You'll need it for verification.

Mark: Good tip, thanks! I was thinking I'd just **fill out** the application online, but I guess I should double-check what they need. I've been meaning to **sort out** a few other things too, like setting up automatic payments for my bills.

Lily: Yeah, getting everything set up right from the start will save you so much hassle later. And if you don't mind me asking, do you plan to **go for** a checking or a savings account?

Mark: Probably a checking account for now. I like the idea of being able to **dip into** my savings whenever I need it, but I'll still have a separate savings account for emergencies.

Lily: Sounds like a solid plan. You'll definitely want to **stay on top of** everything. Let me know if you need help with anything. I've **been through** the process before, so I can give you some pointers.

Mark: Thanks, I might take you up on that! I really want to **wrap this up** soon, so I can focus on other things.

Lily: No problem! Let me know how it goes. I'm sure it'll all **work out** just fine.

Glossary

Figure out: To solve or understand something.

Open up: To start or create something, like an account.

Starting fresh: Beginning something new, without any prior baggage.

Take care of: To handle or manage something.

Look into: To investigate or research something.

Offer up: To provide or present something.

Stop by: To visit briefly.

Check out: To look at something to evaluate it.

Bring along: To take something with you.
Fill out: To complete a form or document.
Sort out: To resolve or organize something.
Go for: To choose something.
Dip into: To use part of a resource, usually savings.
Stay on top of: To keep track of or manage something effectively.
Been through: To experience or go through something.
Wrap this up: To finish or complete something.
Work out: To resolve or turn out well.

Speaking time

Have you ever opened a bank account? What was the process like for you?

If you were to change your bank, what factors would you consider before making a decision?

Understanding Different Payment Systems

Samantha: Hey, Chris! Have you **caught up** with the new payment systems that have been popping up everywhere?

Chris: Oh, hey, Samantha! Yeah, I've been hearing a lot about them. It seems like people are **switching over** to digital wallets more and more. I'm not really sure how they **work out**, though.

Samantha: Same here. I've been trying to **wrap my head around** all the options. There's Apple Pay, Google Pay, Venmo, and even cryptocurrency now. It's a lot to keep track of!

Chris: For sure. I tried using Venmo once, but I wasn't sure how to **set it up** properly. I kept **running into** problems with linking my bank account.

Samantha: Ugh, I know the feeling. But once you get everything **figured out**, it's super easy to use. I **switched to** Apple Pay last year, and it's been a game-changer. You just **tap into** your phone, and boom, you're done.

Chris: That's what I've heard. It's convenient, right? You don't even need to carry a wallet around. But I've also heard some people don't **trust** digital wallets as much. They're worried about security.

Samantha: I get that. But if you take the time to **set up** two-factor authentication, it makes things a lot more secure. I **signed up for** Google Pay recently, and I feel pretty confident about it now. You just have to **stay on top of** your account settings.

Chris: That's a good point. I've been thinking about **looking into** it more, but I don't know if I'm ready to fully **give up** cash just yet. There's something about having physical money on hand that feels more reliable.

Samantha: I get that too, but honestly, I don't even carry cash anymore. I've **fallen into** the habit of paying everything through my phone, and it's just so convenient. I **set it up** to automatically pay bills, so I don't have to worry about late fees.

Chris: Wow, that sounds pretty convenient. Maybe I'll try to **catch up** with the times and give it a go. But I'll probably **start off** slow—just use it for small purchases at first.

Samantha: That's a smart way to go. You can always **back out** if it doesn't work for you. But I think once you **get the hang of** it, you'll love it.

Glossary
Catch up: To become informed about something, often after being behind.
Switching over: Changing from one system to another.
Work out: To turn out successfully or as planned.

Wrap my head around: To understand something complicated or difficult.
Set up: To arrange or prepare something, like an account or device.
Running into: Encountering a problem or difficulty.
Figured out: Solved or understood something.
Switched to: Moved from one thing to another.
Tap into: To access or use something, often electronically.
Trust: To rely on something or someone with confidence.
Stay on top of: To manage or monitor something closely.
Signed up for: Registered or enrolled in something.
Looking into: Investigating or researching something.
Give up: To stop using or doing something.
Fallen into: To have developed a habit or routine.
Catch up with: To update or become current with something.
Start off: To begin something.
Back out: To withdraw or decide not to continue with something.
Get the hang of: To become familiar or comfortable with something.

Speaking time

What payment system do you use most often, and how easy or difficult was it to set up?

Do you think digital wallets are the future, or will cash always be around in some form?

Paying Bills

Jordan: Hey, Sarah! How's everything going?
Sarah: Oh, hey Jordan! I'm good, just **trying to keep up** with all these bills. I can't believe it's already the end of the month.
Jordan: I know, right? The bills always seem to **pile up** this time of year. I was just thinking I need to **pay off** my electricity bill before it's too late.
Sarah: Same here! I've been meaning to **set up** automatic payments, but I always forget. It would definitely help me **stay on top of** everything.
Jordan: That's a good idea. I finally **got around to** doing that last month, and it's made life so much easier. Now I don't even have to worry about it anymore. The payments **just go through** automatically.
Sarah: That sounds awesome. I've been kind of putting it off because I don't want to **mess up** and end up overpaying or something.
Jordan: I get it, but if you **check in** on it every once in a while, you'll be fine. I've had it set up for a while, and it's worked out great. Plus, I never have to **stress over** missing a payment again.
Sarah: That's true. I need to **get on top of** this. Do you use any apps to help with paying your bills?

Jordan: Yeah, I use this app that tracks all my bills and reminds me when they're due. It's been a real lifesaver. You should totally **check it out**.

Sarah: I might! I'll definitely **look into** it. For now, though, I'll just **pay off** my phone bill. I don't want to wait until the last minute.

Jordan: Good call. You don't want to end up with a late fee. I used to do that all the time before I **set up** my bills to be paid automatically.

Sarah: I know, it's so easy to **fall behind**. I think I'll finally **take the plunge** and set it all up today.

Jordan: You won't regret it. Trust me, it'll save you a lot of hassle down the road.

Glossary

Trying to keep up: Attempting to stay on track with something.

Pile up: To accumulate over time, often causing stress.

Pay off: To fully pay something, like a bill.

Set up: To arrange or establish something, like automatic payments.

Stay on top of: To manage or monitor something carefully.

Got around to: Finally doing something after delaying it.

Go through: To complete or process automatically.

Mess up: To make a mistake or cause a problem.

Check in: To review or monitor something periodically.
Stress over: To worry excessively about something.
Get on top of: To manage something effectively or stay organized.
Check it out: To look at or explore something.
Look into: To investigate or research something.
Pay off: To settle a debt or bill.
Set up: To organize or arrange something in advance.
Fall behind: To fall behind schedule or not keep up with something.
Take the plunge: To make a decision to do something, especially after hesitating.

Speaking time

How do you usually handle paying your bills? Do you prefer to pay them manually or set up automatic payments?
What would you do if you accidentally **fell behind** on a bill? How would you **get back on track**?

Talking About Financial Goals

Tom: Hey, Lisa! What's up?
Lisa: Not much, just **thinking about** my financial goals for the next year. I really need to **get a handle on** my spending.
Tom: I hear you! I've been trying to **cut back on** unnecessary expenses too. Have you started **setting up** a budget yet?
Lisa: Yeah, I've started working on it. I want to **save up** for a vacation and build an emergency fund. But it's tough. I keep **falling into** old habits of splurging on small things.
Tom: That's always the challenge! I've been trying to **stick to** a budget for a while now, but it's hard when you want to treat yourself every now and then.
Lisa: Exactly! But I've realized I need to **cut out** some things, like eating out as much. If I **save up** a little every month, I can make it work.
Tom: Good idea. I've been putting money into a savings account every month, even if it's just a little. It's amazing how quickly it starts to **add up** over time.

Lisa: Yeah, I've been reading a lot about the importance of **putting aside** some money, even if it's a small amount. It makes a huge difference in the long run.

Tom: Definitely! And don't forget to **set aside** some for retirement. I've been trying to **build up** my 401(k) plan. It feels good knowing I'm **taking care of** my future.

Lisa: That's a smart move. I need to **look into** retirement plans soon. I'm also thinking about **paying off** my credit card debt by the end of the year. It'll be a huge weight off my shoulders.

Tom: That's a solid goal. I've been trying to **pay down** my student loans, so I'm focusing on that first. But once I'm done, I'll definitely **shift gears** and focus more on saving.

Lisa: It's all about priorities. I think once I **get ahead of** my debt, I'll feel a lot more comfortable **setting aside** extra money for things I really want.

Tom: Exactly! And if you stick to your plan, you'll **be set**. Financial goals are all about consistency.

Lisa: Thanks for the encouragement, Tom. I feel more motivated now. I just need to **stay on track** and not get sidetracked by impulse buys!

Tom: You got it! You'll definitely **pull it off**. Just keep your eyes on the prize!

Glossary
Thinking about: Considering or planning something.

Get a handle on: To gain control or understanding of something.
Cut back on: To reduce or limit something.
Setting up: Organizing or arranging something in advance.
Save up: To accumulate money for a specific purpose.
Falling into: Returning to a bad habit or pattern.
Stick to: To continue doing something consistently.
Cut out: To stop doing something entirely.
Add up: To accumulate over time, usually in a positive way.
Put aside: To reserve or save something for a future purpose.
Set aside: To save or keep something for a specific purpose.
Build up: To gradually increase or accumulate something.
Taking care of: Managing or planning for something important.
Look into: To investigate or research something.
Pay off: To completely settle a debt or obligation.
Pay down: To reduce the balance of a debt.
Shift gears: To change direction or focus.
Get ahead of: To progress beyond or catch up with something.
Be set: To be in a good or stable position.
Stay on track: To continue progressing towards a goal without getting distracted.

Pull it off: To successfully complete something difficult or challenging.

Speaking time
What are your financial goals for the next year? How do you plan to achieve them?
Have you ever tried setting up a budget? How did it go, and what advice would you give someone starting out?

Changing Money

Alex: Hey, Sara, have you ever **changed money** at the airport before?
Sara: Yeah, I have. I usually just **exchange** a little at the airport for convenience, but the rates aren't great. Have you?
Alex: I did once, but I **got ripped off**. They gave me such a bad rate. Now, I **stick to** changing money at a local exchange shop. It's usually way better.
Sara: Oh, I get it. The airport places always seem to **charge** so much more. But sometimes it's just easier to **deal with** it there. I'm planning a trip soon and I need to **figure out** where to change my dollars.
Alex: I totally hear you. I always **take into account** the fees. Sometimes it's worth going to a bank, but you have to **watch out for** hidden fees. They can really add up.

Sara: Yeah, I've heard that. I was thinking about using a card for the exchange, but I've heard the banks **mark up** the exchange rate when you use a credit card abroad.

Alex: Definitely. I try to **use up** all my foreign cash before I leave, so I don't have to **deal with** the exchange rates at all. But if I have to change it, I usually look for the best rate first.

Sara: Smart move. I've also thought about using an app to **transfer** money before the trip. That way I can **lock in** a rate early. Have you ever tried that?

Alex: I have! I've used a couple of apps, and they can be really convenient. The rates are often much better, and you can **send over** the money right from your phone. It's way easier than carrying a ton of cash around.

Sara: That sounds so much easier. I'll have to **look into** that. But, what do you usually do if you're stuck with some leftover foreign currency when you get home?

Alex: I usually just **hold onto** it for the next trip. But if I need to **cash in** the leftover money, I go to a local exchange shop. The fees are still not ideal, but at least it's better than nothing.

Sara: Good idea! I'll definitely remember that. Thanks for the tips, Alex. I feel more prepared now.

Alex: No problem, Sara! Just make sure to **watch out for** those fees, and you'll be good to go.

Glossary

Changed money: Exchanged one currency for another.
Exchange: The act of swapping one type of currency for another.
Got ripped off: To be charged unfairly or too much for something.
Stick to: To consistently choose or follow a certain option or method.
Charge: To ask for a specific price, usually related to a fee or cost.
Deal with: To manage or handle a situation or task.
Figure out: To understand or solve a problem.
Take into account: To consider something when making a decision.
Watch out for: To be cautious or aware of potential problems or dangers.
Mark up: To increase the price of something, often more than is reasonable.
Use up: To completely finish something, such as cash or resources.
Send over: To transfer something, like money, to someone or somewhere else.
Lock in: To secure a specific price or rate in advance.
Look into: To investigate or research something.
Hold onto: To keep something for future use.
Cash in: To exchange something (like foreign currency) for its equivalent value.
Watch out for: To be cautious or alert to something that could cause problems.

Speaking time

How do you usually exchange money when you travel? Do you prefer to use an app or change money at a local exchange shop?

What do you do if you end up with leftover foreign currency after your trip?

Winning the Lottery

Mike: Hey, Jen! You'll never guess what happened to me this morning.

Jen: What happened? You look like you're about to **burst out** with excitement!

Mike: I bought a lottery ticket on a whim, and I actually **won**!

Jen: No way! Are you serious? How much did you win?

Mike: I **hit the jackpot**! It's not millions, but I won $50,000.

Jen: Wow, that's incredible! What are you going to do with all that money? I mean, **the sky's the limit**!

Mike: Honestly, I'm still trying to **wrap my head around** it. I never thought I'd actually win, but now that it's real, I've got a ton of things I want to do. I think I'll **pay off** some of my debt first.
Jen: That's smart. You should definitely **take care of** that first. What else are you thinking of doing?
Mike: Well, I'd love to **take a trip** to Europe, maybe Italy or France. It's always been on my bucket list, but I've never had the money for it. This is my chance to finally **live it up**!
Jen: That sounds amazing. I would totally **splurge on** a nice vacation if I had that kind of money. What about saving some for the future?
Mike: Yeah, that's the plan. I'm going to **set aside** a portion for savings and maybe **invest in** some stocks. I don't want to **blow it all** at once.
Jen: Good idea. It's always tempting to **go overboard** when you get a windfall, but being smart about it will make the money last.
Mike: Exactly. I want to make sure I don't **lose sight of** my goals. But at the same time, I can't wait to **treat myself** a little. You know, **live the dream** for a bit.
Jen: Oh, you deserve it! Just don't forget about all of us when you're living large! Haha.
Mike: Don't worry, I'll definitely **hook you up** with something nice. Maybe a vacation to celebrate!
Jen: Haha, you're the best! I can't wait to hear all about it.

Glossary
Burst out: To suddenly express excitement or emotion.
Hit the jackpot: To win a large amount of money, especially in gambling or a lottery.
The sky's the limit: There are no limits or restrictions on what can be achieved.
Wrap my head around: To understand something that is difficult to comprehend.
Pay off: To fully pay a debt or financial obligation.
Take care of: To handle or manage a task or responsibility.
Take a trip: To travel somewhere for leisure or vacation.
Live it up: To enjoy life to the fullest, often in an extravagant way.
Splurge on: To spend a lot of money on something indulgent or luxurious.
Set aside: To reserve or save something, often money, for future use.
Invest in: To put money into something (like stocks or property) to earn a return.
Blow it all: To spend money carelessly or wastefully.
Go overboard: To do something to an extreme degree, often in spending or actions.
Lose sight of: To forget or become distracted from important goals or priorities.
Treat myself: To indulge or do something special for oneself.
Live the dream: To live an ideal or highly desirable lifestyle.

Hook you up: To give someone something, usually as a gift or favor.

Speaking time
If you won a large amount of money in the lottery, what would be the first thing you would do?

Do you think it's important to save or invest money, even if you win a lot all at once? Why or why not?

Business Bookkeeping

Evan: Hey, Lucy! I've been trying to **sort out** my business finances, and I'm starting to feel a bit overwhelmed. How do you **keep track of** everything?

Lucy: Oh, I totally get it. It's easy to **fall behind** if you don't stay on top of it. I use accounting software to **keep tabs on** all the transactions, but at the end of the day, it's all about **staying organized**.

Evan: Yeah, I'm thinking about using software too, but I'm not sure where to **start out**. There are so many options! How do you **set up** everything?

Lucy: I'd recommend starting with something simple. QuickBooks is great for small businesses. Once you **get the hang of** it, you'll see how much easier it makes managing your books. You just need to **input** your income and expenses regularly.

Evan: Sounds pretty straightforward. I've been trying to **stay on top of** things manually, but I always seem to **fall behind**. I guess I need to **figure out** a better system.

Lucy: I've been there! The key is to **set aside** some time each week to update everything. That way, you don't **get behind** and end up scrambling at the end of the month. I also like to **double-check** my work to make sure there are no mistakes.

Evan: That's smart. I've had some issues with missing receipts before. Do you ever **run into** any problems with that?

Lucy: Oh, all the time! What I do is **keep track of** receipts digitally. I just take pictures of them with my phone and **upload** them straight to the software. It saves a lot of time and hassle.

Evan: That's a great idea. I think I need to **set up** something like that. What about taxes? How do you **deal with** them?

Lucy: I always **make sure to** set aside money for taxes each month. It's easy to **forget about** it, but if you're not careful, you can get in trouble when tax season rolls around. I also **work with** an accountant to make sure everything's in order.

Evan: That makes sense. I've been trying to **work out** a plan for my taxes, but I haven't gotten around to it yet. I guess I should **get on top of** it soon.

Lucy: Absolutely! The earlier you **get ahead of** it, the easier it will be later. You don't want to **rush through** it when the deadline's approaching.

Evan: Yeah, you're right. Thanks for all the tips, Lucy. I think I'm finally starting to **figure out** how to manage my bookkeeping.

Lucy: You're welcome! Just **stay consistent**, and you'll be all set.

Glossary

Sort out: To organize or solve something, especially a problem or task.
Keep track of: To monitor or record information.
Fall behind: To fail to keep up with something, especially tasks or deadlines.
Keep tabs on: To monitor or keep a close eye on something.
Staying organized: Keeping things structured and in order to avoid confusion.
Start out: To begin a process or task.
Set up: To arrange or prepare something for use.

Get the hang of: To become familiar or skilled at something.
Input: To enter information into a system or software.
Stay on top of: To manage something well and ensure it is done regularly.
Fall behind: To lag behind or fail to stay current with something.
Figure out: To understand or solve a problem.
Set aside: To reserve or save something for a specific purpose.
Double-check: To verify or review something for accuracy.
Run into: To encounter or experience a problem.
Keep track of: To record or manage information.
Upload: To transfer data from a local device to an online system.
Deal with: To handle or manage something, especially a difficult task.
Make sure to: To ensure that something is done or achieved.
Forget about: To not remember or fail to consider something important.
Work with: To collaborate or cooperate with someone.
Work out: To figure out or solve a problem.
Get on top of: To gain control or manage something efficiently.
Get ahead of: To take action early, before a problem becomes bigger.

Rush through: To complete something quickly and carelessly.
Figure out: To understand or find a solution to something.
Stay consistent: To continue doing something regularly or without interruption.

Speaking time

How do you keep track of your personal finances? Do you use any specific tools or methods?

What are some challenges you've faced when managing finances, and how did you overcome them?

Get-Rich-Quick Schemes

Sarah: Hey, Jake, have you ever heard about those **get-rich-quick schemes** that seem to pop up everywhere?

Jake: Oh, definitely! I've had people **push** them on me before. They always promise huge returns, but I'm pretty sure they're just trying to **cash in** on people's desperation.

Sarah: Yeah, I've been **bombarded with** emails and social media ads about making easy money from home. They all look so tempting, but I'm really skeptical. I'm afraid I'd just **fall for** a scam.

Jake: Exactly! It's like they **lure you in** with these unbelievable claims, but in the end, they just want you to **hand over** your money. I've learned to **stay clear of** those things. It's just too risky.

Sarah: I know, right? Some of them even try to **pressure** you into making decisions fast, like, "Don't miss out, this offer won't last!" That's always a red flag for me.

Jake: That's a big sign you should **watch out for**. If something sounds too good to be true, it probably is. I've also had friends **talk up** certain "opportunities," but when I really looked into them, they were all just **hype**.

Sarah: Oh, I hate it when people **talk up** things like that. It's like they're trying to **drag you in**. I'd rather **stick to** tried-and-true methods to make money, even if it takes longer.

Jake: Same here. I'd rather **build up** a solid business or investment strategy slowly than try to **hit it big** in one fell swoop. Patience always pays off in the long run.

Sarah: I agree. I'd rather **take my time** and **work towards** my financial goals than risk everything on something that could easily **fall apart**.

Jake: Absolutely. If it doesn't feel right, just **back off** and **move on**. There are plenty of ways to **make money** the honest way.

Sarah: Totally! It's just frustrating how many people get caught up in those schemes and end up losing money. It's better to **go slow** and be careful.

Jake: Couldn't have said it better myself. **Don't fall for** the shortcuts. The real money comes from hard work and smart decisions, not from trying to **cash in** on some fast fix.

Glossary

Get-rich-quick schemes: Plans or methods that promise to make you a lot of money very quickly, often with little effort or investment.

Push: To try to sell or convince someone to do something, often aggressively.

Cash in: To take advantage of a situation to make money, often in a way that benefits only one party.

Bombarded with: To be overwhelmed or constantly exposed to something, usually advertising or messages.

Fall for: To be tricked or deceived by something.

Lure you in: To attract or entice someone into a situation, often under false pretenses.
Hand over: To give something, especially money, to someone.
Stay clear of: To avoid something or someone, especially when it's risky or harmful.
Pressure: To force or coerce someone into making a decision quickly.
Watch out for: To be cautious or aware of potential danger or trickery.
Talk up: To praise or promote something, often exaggerating its value or benefits.
Hype: Exaggerated publicity or promotion of something.
Drag you in: To involve someone in something, often against their better judgment.
Stick to: To continue doing something that is reliable or proven to work.
Build up: To gradually develop or grow something over time.
Hit it big: To become very successful or wealthy suddenly.
Take my time: To proceed slowly and thoughtfully, without rushing.
Work towards: To make progress on a goal or objective over time.
Fall apart: To break down or fail, often suddenly or disastrously.
Back off: To stop pushing or pressuring someone, or to distance yourself from something.
Move on: To stop focusing on something and shift your attention elsewhere.
Go slow: To proceed cautiously or gradually.

Make money: To earn or generate income.
Don't fall for: To avoid being tricked or deceived by something.
Cash in: To make money from a situation, often in a way that is opportunistic.

Speaking time

Have you ever been tempted by a get-rich-quick scheme? What made you decide whether to go for it or not?

In your opinion, what are the most reliable ways to build wealth over time?

A Mistake in the Hotel Bill

Tom: Hey, Jen, I think there's been a **mix-up** with my hotel bill. I just checked out, and they charged me for two extra nights that I didn't even stay!

Jen: Oh no, that's frustrating! Have you **brought it up** with the front desk yet?

Tom: Yeah, I tried to **point it out** when I was checking out, but the receptionist just said to **wait up** and they'd look into it later. I feel like they're just **passing the buck**.

Jen: Ugh, that's the worst. You should definitely **follow up** with them if they don't **sort it out** right away. No way should you be stuck with those extra charges.

Tom: I totally agree. I even asked for an itemized bill to **go over** everything, and there were several charges I don't remember **signing off on**. I think someone just **messed up**.

Jen: That sounds like a mistake on their part. You should also **get in touch** with their manager and see if they can **clear this up**. If it's their error, they should **take care of** it.

Tom: Yeah, I'm planning to. I just don't want to **drag this out** too long. I'm already on my way to the airport and don't want to **waste time** dealing with this.

Jen: I hear you. But if you don't **push back**, they might just **let it slide**. It's better to **sort it out** now than have it **come back** later.

Tom: True. I guess I'll give them a call and **follow through**. Hopefully, they'll **sort it out** and refund me for the extra charges.

Jen: I'm sure they'll fix it. It's just a matter of **getting it straightened out**. Good luck!

Tom: Thanks, Jen. I'll let you know how it goes. Hopefully, they'll **sort things out** without any more trouble.

Glossary

Mix-up: A misunderstanding or mistake, often involving confusion or wrong information.

Brought it up: To raise or mention something, especially an issue or concern.

Point it out: To highlight or draw attention to something specific.

Wait up: To delay or pause, usually for a short time.

Passing the buck: To shift responsibility to someone else.

Follow up: To take further action to resolve an issue or situation.

Sort it out: To resolve or fix a problem or situation.

Go over: To review or examine something carefully.

Signing off on: To approve or authorize something.

Messed up: To make a mistake or cause confusion.

Get in touch: To contact or communicate with someone.

Clear this up: To resolve confusion or misunderstandings.

Take care of: To handle or deal with something, often a problem.
Drag this out: To prolong or delay something unnecessarily.
Waste time: To use time ineffectively or in an unproductive way.
Let it slide: To ignore or overlook a problem, usually because it seems minor.
Follow through: To complete an action or plan.
Get it straightened out: To resolve a situation and make it correct.
Sort things out: To solve problems and make things right.

Speaking time
Have you ever experienced a mistake in a hotel bill? How did you handle it?
What do you think is the best way to deal with mistakes in bills or payments when traveling?

The Supermarket Checkout

Alice: Hey, Mark, do you ever get frustrated with the supermarket checkout? I always seem to **run into** problems when I'm paying.

Mark: Oh, definitely. I was just there this morning and the cashier had to **ring up** my items twice because the scanner wasn't working properly. It was so annoying.

Alice: Ugh, that's the worst! I always end up **holding up** the line when I forget to **grab** something, like I'll be halfway through checking out and realize I missed something from the cart.

Mark: Yeah, I've done that too. I hate **having to go back** for something. And then when you get to the register, sometimes they don't even **ask for** your coupons, and I always **feel bad** when I have to **pull them out** at the last minute.

Alice: Oh, I do that all the time! It's like, "Why didn't I **think of** this sooner?" And don't even get me started on when they **mess up** the prices. I had a can of soup that was marked on sale, but the cashier **rang it up** at the full price. I had to **speak up** about it.

Mark: That's so frustrating. I'm always a little **embarrassed** when I have to **point it out**, but hey, it's their mistake. I usually just **hold off** on paying until they fix it.

Alice: Same here. I don't mind **standing up for** myself in those situations. And then, of course, there's the classic moment when they **forget to bag** your stuff, and you have to **ask them** to finish it.

Mark: Yep, I've definitely **run into** that before. Sometimes I just end up **grabbing** the bags myself. But all in all, it's nice when things **go smoothly** and I can **check out** without any issues.

Alice: Totally! I'll take those days anytime. But it's kind of funny how we **get used to** all the little glitches at the checkout and just **roll with** them, you know?

Mark: Exactly. It's part of the experience. As long as we don't end up **getting charged** for something we didn't buy, I guess we can **live with** the minor annoyances.

Glossary
Run into: To encounter or experience something unexpectedly, often a problem.
Ring up: To scan or record the price of items at a checkout.
Hold up: To delay or cause a delay.
Grab: To take or pick up something quickly.
Having to go back: To return to a previous location or step.
Ask for: To request something.
Feel bad: To feel guilty or apologetic about something.
Pull them out: To take something from a bag, pocket, or place, usually quickly.
Think of: To remember or recall something.

Mess up: To make a mistake or cause confusion.
Speak up: To voice your opinion or point out an issue.
Embarrassed: Feeling self-conscious or ashamed, especially in a social situation.
Point it out: To highlight or draw attention to something, often an error.
Hold off: To delay doing something until a later time.
Stand up for: To defend or support yourself or someone else.
Forget to bag: To fail to put items into bags after they've been purchased.
Run into: To encounter or face a problem or situation.
Grabbing: Taking something quickly and often without much thought.
Go smoothly: To happen without problems or interruptions.
Check out: To complete a purchase at a register.
Get used to: To become familiar with or accustomed to something over time.
Roll with: To adapt to or accept a situation, even if it's not ideal.
Getting charged: Being billed for something, often incorrectly.
Live with: To accept or endure something, even if it's not perfect.

Speaking time

Have you ever experienced a frustrating checkout situation at the supermarket? How did you handle it?

What do you think is the most important thing to remember when shopping at a supermarket checkout?

Asking for a Raise

Tom: Hey, Sarah, I've been thinking a lot about asking for a raise. I've been with the company for a while now, and I feel like it's time to **bring it up** with my boss. What do you think?

Sarah: Oh, I think it's a great idea! But have you already **figured out** what you're going to say? You don't want to just **bring it up** out of nowhere. You need to have your reasons lined up.

Tom: Yeah, that's what I'm worried about. I've been doing a lot of extra work lately, and I've really been trying to **go above and beyond**. I'm just not sure how to **go about** bringing it up without sounding too pushy.

Sarah: You definitely want to **ease into** it. Maybe start by talking about your recent accomplishments and how you've really **stepped up**. Then you can **bring up** your salary and how you feel it doesn't match your contributions.

Tom: Good idea. I guess I should also **take into account** the company's financial situation before I **jump into** the conversation. I don't want to seem out of touch.

Sarah: Exactly, you don't want to **put them on the spot**. Maybe you can **set up** a meeting with your boss to discuss your role and how you've been **killing it** lately. Then, if the conversation goes well, you can **bring up** the raise.

Tom: I like that idea. I think I'll **bring it up** when I've had a chance to **follow up** on some of the projects I've been handling. I don't want to **jump the gun** too soon.

Sarah: Yeah, definitely don't **rush into** it. But at the same time, if you feel like you've earned it, you should **ask for** what you deserve. Just make sure you **back up** your request with facts and examples.

Tom: That's the plan. I'll **prepare** a little more and then **ask for** the raise next week. Thanks for the advice, Sarah. I'll let you know how it goes.

Sarah: No problem! Good luck, Tom. You've definitely earned it, and I'm sure your boss will **appreciate** the conversation.

Glossary

Bring it up: To mention or raise a topic for discussion.

Figure out: To understand or decide how to handle something.

Go above and beyond: To put in extra effort or do more than what is expected.

Go about: To approach or handle something in a particular way.

Ease into: To introduce a topic gently or gradually.

Step up: To take on more responsibility or improve performance.

Take into account: To consider something when making a decision.

Jump into: To start something suddenly or without preparation.

Put them on the spot: To create a situation where someone feels uncomfortable or pressured.
Set up: To arrange or schedule a meeting or event.
Killing it: Doing extremely well, performing excellently.
Follow up: To check in or revisit a topic or situation.
Jump the gun: To act prematurely, without waiting for the right moment.
Rush into: To do something too quickly, without proper consideration.
Ask for: To request something.
Back up: To support or justify a request with facts or evidence.
Prepare: To get ready, usually with necessary information or strategy.
Appreciate: To value or acknowledge something positively.

Speaking time
Have you ever asked for a raise at work? What did you say during the conversation?
What advice would you give someone who is preparing to ask for a raise?

Understanding Interest Rates

John: Hey, Lisa, I've been trying to **wrap my head around** these interest rates for a loan I'm thinking about taking out. It's really confusing!

Lisa: I know what you mean. When I first started looking into loans, I had to **figure out** how the rates worked too. Basically, the higher the interest rate, the more you'll end up paying in the long run.

John: Yeah, that's what I'm worried about. I don't want to **get stuck with** a super high rate and end up paying more than I can handle. How do you **shop around** for the best rate?

Lisa: Good question. The key is to **look into** different options. You can **check out** various banks, credit unions, and even online lenders. Each one may **offer up** different terms, and some might even **cut you a break** if you have a good credit score.

John: I've heard some places will **lock in** a rate for the entire term of the loan. Is that the best option?

Lisa: It can be. If you **lock in** a fixed rate, you won't have to worry about fluctuations in the market. But if you go with a variable rate, it could go up or down depending on market conditions. It's a risk, but sometimes the starting rate can be lower.

John: Hmm, that's a tough call. I guess I should **take into account** my ability to pay back the loan over time, right? I don't want to end up **falling behind** on payments if the rate goes up.

Lisa: Exactly. You need to **think ahead** and make sure you can handle it, especially if the rate **creeps up** over time. You should also **watch out for** any hidden fees that might come with the loan.

John: Hidden fees? That sounds sketchy. What should I **look out for**?

Lisa: Some loans come with processing fees, late fees, or prepayment penalties. You should always **read the fine print** before signing anything so you don't end up paying more than you expected.

John: Got it. I'll definitely **look into** all that. I just want to make sure I don't **get in over my head** with this loan.

Lisa: Yeah, that's the key. Take your time and **weigh all your options**. Don't rush into it.

John: Thanks, Lisa. I feel a lot more confident now that I know what to **keep an eye on**. I'll **make sure** to do my homework before I commit.

Glossary

Wrap my head around: To understand something that is complex or difficult.
Figure out: To understand or solve something.
Get stuck with: To be forced to deal with something, often a negative situation.

Shop around: To compare prices or options from different sources before making a decision.
Look into: To investigate or research something.
Check out: To examine or evaluate something.
Offer up: To present or provide something, often as a choice.
Cut you a break: To offer a deal or a discount, often as a favor.
Lock in: To secure or fix something, usually a price or rate, for a set period.
Take into account: To consider or factor in something when making a decision.
Falling behind: To fail to keep up with something, such as payments or obligations.
Think ahead: To plan for the future, consider potential outcomes.
Creep up: To gradually increase, often in a subtle or unnoticed way.
Watch out for: To be cautious or aware of something, especially potential risks or problems.
Look out for: To be on the lookout for, to pay attention to.
Read the fine print: To carefully review the detailed terms and conditions of an agreement or contract.
Get in over my head: To become involved in a situation that is too difficult or risky to handle.

Weigh all your options: To carefully consider all available choices before making a decision.
Keep an eye on: To monitor or watch something closely.
Make sure: To ensure something is done correctly or adequately.

Speaking time
What do you think is the most important factor to consider when choosing a loan or credit offer?
Have you ever dealt with a loan or interest rate before? How did you manage the process?

Talking About Wealth

Alice: So, Mike, I've been thinking a lot about wealth lately. It seems like some people **have it all**, while others are just struggling to **get by**. Do you think there's a secret to building wealth?

Mike: Hmm, that's a good question. I think some people **get lucky** and inherit wealth, but for most of us, it's about making smart choices and **building up** assets over time. You can't just expect to **come into** money overnight.

Alice: Right, it's not like you can just **hit the jackpot** every time. But it's tough because, even if you work hard, there's always that fear of **falling behind**. Like, you work hard and save, but prices keep going up, and it feels like you're not making any progress.

Mike: That's true. But you also have to **keep an eye on** where your money is going. If you want to **build wealth**, you need to **cut back on** unnecessary spending. I'm trying to **save up** for a house, so I've really been **cutting back** on things like eating out and buying stuff I don't need.

Alice: That's smart. I've been trying to **set aside** a little bit each month too, but it's hard. Every time I **splurge on** something I really want, it feels like I'm **set back**.

Mike: Yeah, it can be hard to stay disciplined. But the key is to **stick with** your plan and **take control of** your spending. Over time, that can really pay off. I've also been looking into ways to **grow my money** through investments.

Alice: Oh, you mean like stocks or real estate?

Mike: Exactly. I've been trying to **research** different options and **figure out** what makes the most sense for me. I'm not a financial expert, but I know that you can't just **sit on** your savings. You have to **make them work** for you.

Alice: I hear you. But it's hard not to feel like you're **getting ripped off** by some of these investment opportunities. You really have to **do your homework** before diving in.

Mike: Absolutely. You can't just **jump into** anything without understanding the risks. I always **check out** reviews and talk to people who've been in the game longer. That way, I don't end up **throwing away** my money on a bad investment.

Alice: That's smart. I guess the most important thing is to not get too caught up in the idea of **getting rich quick**. It's more about consistency and smart decisions over time.
Mike: Exactly. Building wealth isn't about overnight success; it's about **setting yourself up** for the future. Little by little, it all **adds up**.

Glossary
Have it all: To have everything one could want or need, often referring to wealth or success.
Get by: To manage or survive, usually in difficult circumstances.
Get lucky: To experience good fortune or a lucky break.
Building up: Gradually accumulating or increasing something, often wealth or resources.
Come into: To suddenly acquire, often used in the context of receiving an inheritance or large sum of money.
Hit the jackpot: To have great success or suddenly become very wealthy, usually by chance.
Falling behind: Failing to keep up with progress or others, often in financial terms.
Keep an eye on: To watch or monitor something closely.
Cut back on: To reduce or limit something, often spending.
Save up: To put money aside for a future purpose or goal.

Splurge on: To spend money freely or extravagantly on something.
Set back: To cause delay or hindrance, often referring to finances or progress.
Stick with: To continue doing something despite challenges or difficulties.
Take control of: To manage or assume responsibility for something.
Grow my money: To invest money in a way that increases its value or returns over time.
Sit on: To keep something without using or benefiting from it, especially money or assets.
Make them work: To use resources effectively to achieve a goal, especially with money.
Getting ripped off: Being charged more than something is worth or being deceived financially.
Do your homework: To thoroughly research or prepare before making a decision.
Jump into: To start something without thinking it through completely.
Throwing away: Wasting something, especially money.
Getting rich quick: Trying to become wealthy rapidly, often by taking risks or shortcuts.
Set yourself up: To prepare yourself for future success or stability.
Adds up: To accumulate or build up over time.

Speaking time

Do you believe it's possible to **get rich quick**, or is building wealth more about consistency and smart choices?

What steps do you take to **manage your money** and **build wealth** over time?

Filing Taxes

Sarah: Hey, Tom, I've been putting off filing my taxes, and now the deadline is **creeping up** on me! Do you have any tips on how to **tackle** it without losing my mind?

Tom: Oh, I totally get it! Taxes can be overwhelming. The first thing I always do is **gather up** all my documents—W-2s, receipts, everything I need. You don't want to **miss out** on anything that could lower your bill.

Sarah: Yeah, that's the part I always struggle with. I'm afraid I'll **leave out** some deduction and end up paying more than I should. Do you use an accountant, or do you **handle** it yourself?

Tom: I used to **go through** an accountant, but now I **do it myself** using an online program. It's pretty straightforward once you **get the hang of it**. Plus, it's a lot cheaper than paying someone else.

Sarah: I've thought about doing it myself, but I'm always worried I'll **mess up** and end up in trouble with the IRS. Do you ever **check over** your forms to make sure everything looks right?

Tom: For sure! I always **double-check** everything, especially the numbers. If you're not 100% sure, it's worth taking a little extra time to **go over** everything before you submit it. No point in rushing and getting it wrong.

Sarah: That makes sense. I guess I just need to **get organized** and stop procrastinating. Do you ever **file early** to avoid the last-minute stress?

Tom: Yep, I try to **file early** every year. It's so much less stressful when you're not scrambling at the last minute. And sometimes you can even **get back** your refund faster if you file early.

Sarah: That's a good point. I think I'll try to **get ahead** this year. Maybe it won't be so bad if I just **break it down** into smaller steps.

Tom: Exactly! Just **take it one step at a time**. Once you start, it won't seem as bad as it does when you're putting it off.

Sarah: Thanks, Tom. I feel a lot better about getting started now. I'll **knuckle down** and make sure I have everything ready to go.

Tom: No problem! You've got this. Just don't **let it pile up** next year!

Glossary

Creeping up: Approaching gradually or becoming imminent.
Tackle: To deal with or begin a task or challenge.
Gather up: To collect or assemble things.
Miss out: To fail to include or take advantage of something.
Leave out: To omit or not include something.
Handle: To manage or take care of something.
Go through: To carefully examine or process something.
Get the hang of it: To learn how to do something, especially after some effort or practice.
Mess up: To make a mistake or cause something to go wrong.
Check over: To review or inspect something carefully.
Double-check: To verify or confirm something a second time to ensure accuracy.
Go over: To review something thoroughly.

Get organized: To arrange or structure things in an orderly way.
File early: To submit something, such as taxes, before the deadline.
Get back: To receive something, like a refund, that was previously given.
Get ahead: To make progress or stay ahead of a schedule.
Break it down: To divide something into smaller, more manageable parts.
Take it one step at a time: To handle something gradually, step by step, without rushing.
Knuckle down: To focus and work hard on something.
Let it pile up: To allow tasks or responsibilities to accumulate over time without addressing them.

Speaking time

How do you usually **prepare** for filing taxes?
Do you **prefer** handling it yourself or using an accountant?
What strategies do you use to **stay organized** when you have to deal with important tasks?

Talking About Prices

Megan: Hey, Mark! I was shopping for a new laptop yesterday, and I noticed the prices have really **gone up** in the last year. Have you noticed that too?

Mark: Yeah, it's crazy. I remember when you could **pick up** a decent laptop for under $500, and now you're looking at at least $700 for something with good specs. It's like they've **jacked up** the prices for no reason!

Megan: I know! And I'm not even talking about the high-end models. The mid-range ones have **shot up** in price. It's hard to **keep up with** these changes. I feel like I need to **break down** my budget just to afford some of these gadgets.

Mark: It's definitely tough. But I guess when demand **goes up**, prices follow suit. Have you tried to **shop around** for deals? Sometimes you can find something with a good discount if you **look around** a little bit.

Megan: I have, but even with discounts, the prices still seem a bit high. It feels like the companies are **marking up** everything. Even the cheaper models have prices that seem to **add up** quickly.

Mark: Yeah, I hear you. But you might want to **hold off** on buying for a couple of weeks. Sales are coming up soon, and you could probably **cash in on** a good deal. I always try to **wait for** the holiday sales.

Megan: That's a good idea. I've been thinking about **holding out** for Black Friday. It seems like everything goes on sale then. If I **stick to** my plan, I can probably save a good amount.

Mark: Exactly. If you **hold off** until then, you could **score** a big discount. I've done that with some electronics in the past, and it really pays off. But you've got to **keep an eye on** the deals as soon as they come out. They go fast.

Megan: I'll definitely do that. I'll just **hold out** for a better deal and keep my fingers crossed that prices **go down** a bit.

Mark: That's the way to go! And don't forget to **shop around** for the best price once you decide. Sometimes one store will **knock down** the price more than others.

Megan: Good point. I'll be on the lookout for those deals. Thanks for the tips, Mark!

Glossary

Gone up: Increased, usually in terms of prices or numbers.

Pick up: To buy or acquire something.

Jacked up: Increased, especially when referring to prices that have been raised unfairly or excessively.

Shot up: Increased rapidly.

Keep up with: To stay informed or stay at the same level as something, like changing prices or trends.

Break down: To analyze or separate something into smaller, manageable parts.

Look around: To search or explore different options.

Marking up: Raising the price of something, often above its original value.
Add up: To accumulate or increase, often used when discussing total costs.
Hold off: To delay or postpone something.
Cash in on: To take advantage of an opportunity, especially a financial one.
Wait for: To hold out for something that is expected to happen or appear.
Holding out: Waiting for something better or more advantageous before making a decision.
Stick to: To continue with a plan or decision, without changing course.
Score: To get or acquire something, often used when referring to a good deal or bargain.
Keep an eye on: To monitor something closely.
Go down: To decrease in value or price.
Knock down: To lower or reduce the price of something.

Speaking time
How do you usually **shop around** for the best deals when you need to buy something expensive?
Do you think waiting for sales events, like Black Friday, is a good strategy to **save money** on big purchases? Why or why not?

Using an ATM

Lily: Hey, Mark, I need to **stop by** the ATM to **withdraw** some cash. Have you used one recently? I always seem to **run into** issues with them.

Mark: Oh, yeah, I use ATMs all the time. I usually **go to** the one at the corner of 5th Street, but sometimes they're out of order. Have you checked to see if the one near you is working?

Lily: Actually, I tried to **get money out** earlier today, but it kept saying "insufficient funds" even though I knew there was enough in my account. It was so frustrating! Do you ever **double-check** your balance before using the ATM?

Mark: Yeah, I always **make sure** my balance is okay before I go to the machine. I **check it out** online first just to be safe. That way, I don't get stuck in the middle of a transaction.

Lily: That's a good idea. I usually just **stick in** my card and hope for the best. Maybe I need to **pay more attention** next time. Have you ever had your card **eaten by** an ATM?

Mark: Ugh, yes! That's the worst. I once **had to deal with** it for over an hour. You have to **contact** the bank to get it back. It's such a hassle. It's always best to **keep an eye on** your card when you're using the ATM.

Lily: That sounds terrible. I'll definitely **be more careful** from now on. I don't want to go through that. Do you know if there's a way to **speed up** the process, though? I always feel like it takes forever to **get through** the screens.

Mark: Honestly, I think it's just one of those things we have to **put up with**. But if you **keep it simple**—just go for withdrawing the cash or checking your balance—you can **get through** the process faster. I've gotten pretty good at **skipping over** the extra options.

Lily: I'll try that next time. I always end up **clicking on** the wrong thing and wasting time! Thanks for the tips, Mark. I'll **make sure** to follow your advice.

Mark: No problem! I'm sure you'll be fine next time. Just **keep your wits about you**, and you'll be good to go.

Glossary
Stop by: To visit briefly.
Withdraw: To take money out of a bank account.
Run into: To experience or encounter a problem or difficulty.
Go to: To visit or use a location, such as an ATM.
Get money out: To withdraw money.
Double-check: To verify something a second time for accuracy.
Make sure: To ensure or confirm something is correct or okay.

Check it out: To look at or verify something, typically online or in advance.
Stick in: To insert something, such as a card, into a machine.
Pay more attention: To be more careful or aware of something.
Eaten by: To have something, like a card, taken by a machine.
Deal with: To handle or manage a situation or problem.
Contact: To get in touch with someone, typically for assistance.
Keep an eye on: To watch carefully or pay attention to something.
Be more careful: To act with more caution or attention.
Speed up: To make something happen faster.
Get through: To finish or complete something, like a process or procedure.
Put up with: To tolerate or endure something unpleasant.
Keep it simple: To avoid complicating things unnecessarily.
Skipping over: To bypass or not deal with something.
Clicking on: To press a button or option on a screen.
Make sure: To ensure that something is correct or complete.
Keep your wits about you: To stay alert and aware, especially in situations where you need to be cautious.

Speaking time

Have you ever **run into** any issues while using an ATM? How did you **deal with** it?

What are some ways you can **speed up** the process when using an ATM or other similar machines?

Being Rich and Poor

Sarah: Hey, Tom, I've been thinking a lot about money lately. It's crazy how some people just **seem to have it all**, while others are barely getting by. I mean, does it ever make you wonder how people **end up** so rich?

Tom: Oh, totally. I know people who **come from** nothing but somehow **hit it big**. It's like they just **get lucky** and everything **falls into place** for them. But honestly, I think a lot of it has to do with **sticking to** good habits—working hard, being smart with investments, and **keeping your eyes open** for opportunities.

Sarah: Yeah, you're right. But on the flip side, it's hard not to feel bad for people who **struggle to make ends meet**. It feels like no matter how hard they try, they just can't **get ahead**.

Tom: I get that. There are people who **work their butts off**, but they just can't seem to **catch a break**. It's like they're always **living paycheck to paycheck**. It's tough.

Sarah: Exactly. I feel like, no matter how much you **bust your tail**, sometimes you just can't **catch up**. But I guess that's why a lot of people **turn to** credit cards and loans, just to keep up with bills and stuff.

Tom: Yeah, but that can **get out of hand** fast. People end up **drowning in debt** if they're not careful. The key is really to **cut down on** spending where you can, but I know it's easier said than done.

Sarah: It definitely is. I think if you can **hold onto** even a little bit of savings, it makes a big difference when life throws you a curveball. I've been trying to **set aside** more money each month, but sometimes it's hard to **stick to** the plan.

Tom: I hear you. It's tough to **stay on track** when unexpected things come up. But hey, even small steps can help you **get by**. Have you tried using a budget app? That could help you **keep track of** your spending.

Sarah: I've thought about it. I guess it's just about **making sure** you don't overspend. Like, if you're careful, you can **get by** without too much trouble. But it's harder when the cost of living **goes up** so much, right?

Tom: That's true. With inflation, everything **adds up**. But I guess the goal is to **stay afloat**, right? You can't always be rich, but as long as you're not sinking, you're doing okay.

Sarah: True. It's all about **finding a balance**. Being smart with money, saving a little, and just trying to **get by**. I think that's all we can do.

Glossary
Seem to have it all: Appear to possess everything one wants or needs, especially money or success.
End up: To eventually reach a particular state or condition, often unexpectedly.
Come from: To originate from a certain background or place.
Hit it big: To become very successful, especially financially.
Get lucky: To experience good fortune by chance.
Falls into place: Things working out in a way that seems natural or easy.
Sticking to: To continue following a plan or idea.
Keeping your eyes open: To remain alert for opportunities or changes.
Struggle to make ends meet: To have difficulty earning enough money to cover basic expenses.
Get ahead: To make progress or improve one's financial or personal situation.
Work your butt off: To work extremely hard.
Catch a break: To have something good happen after a period of struggle or difficulty.
Living paycheck to paycheck: To only earn enough money to cover basic expenses, with little to no savings.
Bust your tail: To work very hard.
Catch up: To overcome a delay or deficit, often financially.

Turn to: To seek help or support from something or someone.
Get out of hand: To become uncontrollable or problematic.
Drowning in debt: To have more debt than one can manage.
Cut down on: To reduce or decrease something, such as expenses.
Hold onto: To keep something, especially money or resources.
Set aside: To save something for later use, typically money.
Stick to: To follow through with a plan or decision.
Stay on track: To remain focused or continue following a plan.
Get by: To manage or survive, often in difficult circumstances.
Keep track of: To monitor or record something, such as spending or progress.
Making sure: To ensure or confirm something is done properly.
Go up: To increase in price or amount.
Add up: To accumulate or increase over time.
Stay afloat: To manage financially without going under or failing.
Finding a balance: To achieve a state of stability or equilibrium between different things or priorities.

Speaking time
Have you ever had a time when you had to **work your butt off** just to **get by**? How did you manage?

Do you think it's possible for someone to **catch a break** and suddenly **hit it big**? Why or why not?

Recovering After a Setback

Emma: Hey Jake, I heard about the project. I know it didn't **pan out** the way you wanted it to. How are you doing?
Jake: Yeah, it was a tough break. I **felt down** for a while, but I'm slowly **bouncing back**. I guess sometimes things just don't **go your way**, no matter how much effort you put in.
Emma: I totally get that. It's like you **work your butt off** and then **hit a wall**. It can feel like everything is falling apart. How do you even **pick yourself up** after something like that?
Jake: Honestly, I've just been trying to **take things one day at a time**. It's not easy, but I've learned to **keep my head up** and stay positive. The important thing is to **stay focused** and not let one setback **define** everything.

Emma: That's a good mindset. I think you just have to **shake it off** and **move forward**, even if it feels hard at first. Have you been talking to anyone about it?

Jake: Yeah, I've been **leaning on** a few friends. It helps to **vent** sometimes. I also **take a step back** and look at the bigger picture. A setback doesn't mean it's the end. It's just a part of the journey.

Emma: That's a great way to see it. Sometimes you just need to **step away** from the situation and get some perspective. I know it can be frustrating, but like you said, it's just part of the process.

Jake: Exactly! It's important to **keep your chin up** and **not dwell on** the past. The faster you **let go** of what happened, the quicker you can start **moving on** to the next thing.

Emma: You're absolutely right. It's about **rolling with the punches** and **not letting setbacks get the best of you**. I'm sure you'll **bounce back** stronger than ever.

Jake: Thanks, Emma. I appreciate it. I'm just going to **take it one step at a time** and **see where it takes me**.

Glossary

Pan out: To turn out or result in a particular way, often unexpectedly.

Felt down: To feel sad or discouraged.

Bouncing back: To recover from a setback or difficult situation.

Go your way: To happen in a way you want or expect.

Work your butt off: To work very hard.
Hit a wall: To reach a point where progress is stopped or slowed down significantly.
Pick yourself up: To recover from a setback or difficult situation.
Take things one day at a time: To deal with one problem or situation at a time instead of worrying about everything at once.
Keep your head up: To remain positive and hopeful, even during difficult times.
Stay focused: To maintain attention and concentration on a task or goal.
Shake it off: To recover from a negative experience and move forward.
Move forward: To continue making progress or advancing, especially after a setback.
Leaning on: To rely on someone for support or help.
Vent: To express strong feelings, often frustration or anger, in order to feel better.
Take a step back: To pause and assess the situation objectively.
Step away: To physically or emotionally distance yourself from something to gain perspective.
Keep your chin up: To stay positive, even in difficult situations.
Not dwell on: To avoid thinking about or focusing too much on something negative.
Let go: To stop holding onto something, emotionally or mentally.
Moving on: To move past an issue or event and begin focusing on the future.

Rolling with the punches: To adapt to difficult situations or setbacks.
Not letting setbacks get the best of you: Not allowing challenges or obstacles to defeat you.
Take it one step at a time: To approach a situation slowly and carefully, without rushing.
See where it takes me: To go along with a situation and see what happens.

Speaking time
Can you think of a time when you had to **bounce back** from a setback? How did you **pick yourself up**?
How do you usually **shake off** negative experiences and **keep moving forward** after facing difficulties?

Buying a Luxury Car

Tom: Hey Sarah, I heard you just **splurged** on a new car! Is it really a luxury car?
Sarah: Yeah, I finally decided to **go for it**. I've been thinking about it for months, and I just couldn't **pass up** the chance when I saw it. It's a **dream car**!
Tom: Wow, that's awesome! What made you **pull the trigger** now? I know you were kind of **on the fence** about it before.
Sarah: Well, I've been **saving up** for a while, and after doing some research, I felt it was the right time to **treat myself**. Plus, I've always wanted one, so I thought, why not?

Tom: I get it! It's one of those things you just **can't pass up** once you've made up your mind. So, what's the model? You **went all out**, right?

Sarah: Yep, I went all out! It's a brand-new **Porsche**. The color is amazing, and the interior is just... wow. I feel like I'm **living the dream** every time I get in it.

Tom: That sounds incredible! I'm sure it's a huge upgrade from your old car. Does it feel weird to **show off** a little now?

Sarah: Honestly, it feels great! I'm not usually one to **flash** what I have, but this car is something I've **worked hard for**. I think it's okay to **show off** a bit when it's something that's really special to you, right?

Tom: Absolutely! You've earned it. Just make sure to **take care of it**—those luxury cars can be expensive to maintain. I heard the insurance is crazy too!

Sarah: Yeah, I've heard the same. But I've got a plan to **cover** everything. I'm not going to let a few extra expenses **hold me back** from enjoying it. I'll **figure it out**!

Tom: Smart move. I bet you'll be getting a lot of attention on the road. Just be careful not to **show off too much**. You don't want to attract the wrong kind of attention!

Sarah: Oh, I know! I'll definitely **keep a low profile** when I'm driving it around. But it's nice to **treat yourself** once in a while, you know?

Tom: For sure! You deserve it. I'm happy for you. You've definitely **earned it**.

Glossary
Splurged: To spend a large amount of money on something expensive or luxurious.
Go for it: To make a decision to do something or pursue something you've been thinking about.
Pass up: To refuse or let go of an opportunity.
Pull the trigger: To make a final decision or take action, especially after a period of consideration.
On the fence: Being uncertain or indecisive about something.
Saving up: To accumulate money for a specific purpose or goal over time.
Treat myself: To buy something special for oneself as a reward or indulgence.
Can't pass up: To not be able to resist or let go of an opportunity.
Went all out: To put in maximum effort or spend a lot of money to get something special.
Living the dream: To have or experience something that is ideal or aspirational.
Show off: To display something to attract attention or admiration.
Flash: To show something quickly in order to impress others.
Worked hard for: To achieve something through effort and perseverance.
Take care of it: To maintain or preserve something in good condition.
Cover: To take care of or pay for expenses.
Hold me back: To prevent or stop someone from doing something they want to do.

Figure it out: To solve or understand something.
Show off too much: To excessively display or boast about something.
Keep a low profile: To remain unnoticed or not attract attention.
Treat yourself: To reward yourself with something special.
Earned it: To deserve something based on effort or achievement.

Speaking time

Have you ever made a big purchase that you felt was a **treat yourself** moment? How did it feel to **splurge** like that?

Do you think it's okay to **show off** a little when you've **worked hard for** something, or do you prefer to **keep a low profile**?

Exchanging Rates

Mark: Hey, Julie! I need to **figure out** how much I'm going to get when I **exchange** my euros for dollars. The rate seems to **fluctuate** all the time. Have you checked it recently?

Julie: Oh yeah, I **keep track** of exchange rates. I usually **look up** the rate online before I **make** any exchanges. It's always a good idea to **shop around** a bit, you know?

Mark: Definitely! I was thinking of going to the bank, but I've heard their rates aren't as good. Do you think it's better to **go with** a local exchange service or just **stick with** the bank?

Julie: I'd recommend **going with** a currency exchange service if you can **find one** that offers a better rate. Banks tend to **mark up** their rates to make a profit. But if you **have to** go to the bank, it's better than doing it at the airport—those rates are usually the worst!

Mark: That's a good point. I've heard the airport rates are crazy! I'll definitely **keep an eye on** the rates, especially if I'm going to **exchange** a large amount.

Julie: Yeah, for big amounts, even a small difference in rates can **add up**. If you **plan ahead**, you can usually **save** a good chunk of change. Oh, and don't forget about any transaction fees!

Mark: Right! I'll need to **watch out for** those hidden fees. It can really **throw off** the whole exchange. I'll also make sure to **compare** a few places before I **pull the trigger**.

Julie: Sounds like a solid plan. Also, don't **get stuck** with leftover foreign currency after your trip. You can always **swap** it back or **hold on to** it for your next trip!

Mark: Great advice! Thanks, Julie. I'll definitely **keep this in mind** before I make my decision.

Glossary
Figure out: To understand or calculate something.

Exchange: To trade one currency for another.
Fluctuate: To change or vary, especially in price.
Keep track: To monitor or keep updated on something.
Look up: To search for information.
Make: To perform or carry out an action.
Shop around: To compare prices or services before making a decision.
Go with: To choose or select.
Stick with: To continue with a plan or choice.
Mark up: To increase the price of something.
Have to: To be required to do something.
Keep an eye on: To monitor or pay attention to something.
Add up: To accumulate or total.
Plan ahead: To make arrangements or preparations in advance.
Save: To keep money or resources instead of spending them.
Watch out for: To be careful about something.
Throw off: To cause something to be wrong or unexpected.
Compare: To examine two or more things to find differences.
Pull the trigger: To make a final decision or take action.
Get stuck: To be unable to move forward or progress.
Swap: To exchange one thing for another.
Hold on to: To keep something for future use.
Keep this in mind: To remember or consider something.

Speaking time

Have you ever had to **figure out** the best place to **exchange** money while traveling? What did you do to **get the best deal**?

Do you prefer to **stick with** a familiar exchange service, or do you like to **shop around** for better rates? Why?

Collecting Debt

Tom: Hey, Sarah, I need your advice. I've been trying to **collect** a debt from a client for weeks, but they keep **putting me off**. What should I do?

Sarah: Ugh, that's frustrating. Sounds like they're just **stalling** you. Have you tried **following up** with them again, maybe through email or a formal letter?

Tom: Yeah, I've emailed them a few times, but they just **brush it off** like it's no big deal. I'm thinking of **getting tough** with them and maybe **sending** a final warning letter.

Sarah: That could do the trick. But make sure you **set a deadline** in the letter. Let them know you'll **take further action** if they don't pay up by a certain date.

Tom: That's what I was thinking. I don't want to **escalate** the situation, but I also don't want them to think they can just **get away with** not paying.

Sarah: Right, you can't just let them **walk all over you**. If they still don't respond, you might want to **bring in** a collection agency. They're pretty good at **tracking down** people who owe money.

Tom: Hmm, I didn't want to go that route yet. I feel like that could **turn things around**, but I don't want to make things more awkward. Do you think it's too soon?

Sarah: It depends. If the debt is big enough and they've been **stringing you along**, it might be worth it. But you can always try **working it out** with them first. Maybe there's a way to **negotiate** a payment plan.

Tom: True. I'll give them one last chance to **sort things out** on their own. If that doesn't work, I guess I'll have to **take legal action**.

Sarah: I hear you. Hopefully, it won't come to that, but it's always good to **know your options**. Just don't let them **drag you out** for too long.

Tom: Thanks, Sarah. I'll **keep my fingers crossed** they pay up without any more hassle.

Glossary
Collect: To gather or receive payment for something owed.
Putting me off: Delaying or avoiding something.
Stalling: To delay or procrastinate on something.
Following up: To check back or contact someone again.
Brush it off: To dismiss or ignore something.
Get tough: To adopt a firmer or stricter approach.
Set a deadline: To establish a time limit for something.
Take further action: To take additional steps, often legal, in a situation.
Escalate: To increase the intensity or seriousness of a situation.
Get away with: To avoid punishment or consequences.
Walk all over you: To take advantage of someone.
Bring in: To involve someone or something, like a professional or service.
Tracking down: Finding someone, often in difficult situations.

Stringing you along: To deceive someone by making false promises or delaying action.
Working it out: To resolve a problem or situation.
Negotiate: To discuss terms or conditions to come to an agreement.
Sort things out: To resolve a problem or confusion.
Take legal action: To pursue legal steps, such as filing a lawsuit.
Know your options: To understand the different choices available to you.
Drag you out: To delay something unnecessarily or for too long.
Keep my fingers crossed: To hope for a good outcome.

Speaking time

Have you ever had to **collect** a debt or **chase down** someone for payment? What strategy did you use?

If someone kept **stalling** you on a payment, would you **take legal action** right away, or would you try to **work it out** first? Why?

Giving Correct Change

Jane: Hey, Mark, I had the strangest experience at the store today. I bought a coffee, and the cashier gave me **wrong change**.

Mark: Oh no! That's always annoying. What happened? Did they **mess up** the math or something?

Jane: Yeah, exactly. I handed over a $20 bill, and the total was $6.50. The cashier gave me back $8.50 instead of $13.50!

Mark: Yikes, that's a big mistake! Did you **point it out** to them right away?

Jane: I did. I told them they made a mistake, and they **kind of shrugged it off** at first. But when I showed them the receipt, they realized they had **messed up**.

Mark: Good thing you **caught that**! I guess sometimes people are in a rush and don't **pay attention** when giving change.

Jane: Yeah, for sure. They were **rushing through** the line, and I guess it slipped through. But it got me thinking, why don't cashiers always **double-check** the change before handing it over?

Mark: You're right. It only takes a second to **look over** the amount. I always **count my change** to make sure it adds up.

Jane: Same here! I've had a few times where I **didn't realize** the mistake until I was already out the door, and I had to **go back**.

Mark: Ugh, that's the worst. But I guess it's always good to **speak up** if there's an error. I've seen people just **let it slide**, but that's not a good habit.

Jane: Exactly. It's important to be **honest** about it, and I know I'd want someone to do the same for me. After all, it's not just about money; it's about being fair.

Mark: Absolutely. It's all about **getting it right** the first time and not making mistakes. At least the cashier **fixed it** right away!

Glossary
Wrong change: When the amount of money given back is incorrect.
Mess up: To make a mistake or do something incorrectly.
Point it out: To mention or highlight something.
Shrug it off: To dismiss something as unimportant.
Caught that: To notice or realize something.
Pay attention: To focus or be careful about something.
Rushing through: To do something quickly, often without paying full attention.
Double-check: To verify or check something again for accuracy.
Look over: To examine something carefully.
Count my change: To verify the amount of money received.
Didn't realize: To not notice or become aware of something.
Go back: To return to a previous location or point.
Speak up: To say something, usually to correct a mistake or share an opinion.
Let it slide: To ignore or overlook something, often a mistake.
Be honest: To tell the truth or be straightforward.
Getting it right: To do something correctly.

Fixed it: To correct or solve a problem.

Speaking time
Have you ever been given **wrong change** at a store? How did you **handle it**?

When you receive change, do you usually **count it** right away, or do you wait until later? Why?

Spending Money

Sarah: Hey, Mark, I've been trying to **cut back** on my spending lately. I feel like I've been **blowing money** left and right on stuff I don't really need.

Mark: I know what you mean. It's so easy to **give in** to impulse buys. But once you **take a look** at your bank account, it's like, "Whoa, I've spent way more than I thought!"

Sarah: Exactly! I've been trying to **stick to** a budget, but it's hard when I see things I really want. Yesterday, I almost **caved in** and bought a new jacket, even though I don't need it.

Mark: Oh man, that sounds familiar. But honestly, sometimes it feels good to **splurge** every once in a while. You work hard, and you deserve it, right?

Sarah: True, but I've been **falling behind** on saving for a trip I want to take. If I don't **tighten up** my spending, I won't have enough money.

Mark: Yeah, I get that. I've been trying to **save up** for a new car, so I'm being more careful with what I spend. I try to **think twice** before buying something, like, "Do I really need this?"

Sarah: That's a good idea. I should definitely **think things through** before making a purchase. I just get so caught up in the moment sometimes.

Mark: Totally! It's all about finding that balance between treating yourself and not going overboard. If you **keep track** of your spending, it's easier to **stay on top** of your budget.

Sarah: You're right. I need to **scale back** a bit. It's all about being smart with where I put my money. If I **hold off** on some small purchases, I can make bigger plans in the future.

Mark: Exactly! You've got this. Just remember to **hold back** when you're tempted to splurge. Your future self will thank you.

Glossary

Cut back: To reduce or decrease something, usually expenses or consumption.

Blowing money: Spending money carelessly or irresponsibly.

Give in: To surrender or yield to temptation or pressure.

Take a look: To examine or review something.

Caved in: To give up or succumb to temptation.

Splurge: To spend money freely or extravagantly, usually on something not necessary.

Falling behind: To fail to keep up or make progress, especially in saving or goals.

Tighten up: To become more strict or controlled, especially in spending or budget.

Save up: To accumulate money for a specific purpose over time.

Think twice: To reconsider or evaluate something carefully before making a decision.

Think things through: To carefully consider the consequences of a decision or action.

Keep track: To monitor or record something, like spending or progress.

Stay on top: To maintain control or manage something well.

Scale back: To reduce or decrease in size, amount, or extent.

Hold off: To delay or postpone doing something.
Hold back: To resist or refrain from doing something.

Speaking time

What's the last thing you **splurged** on? Do you think it was worth it?

How do you usually **scale back** your spending when you're trying to save up for something important?

Different Payment Systems

Anna: Hey, Mark, I've been thinking about switching to a different payment system. I usually just **stick with** my credit card, but I keep hearing about these new digital wallets. Have you ever **tried out** something like that?

Mark: Yeah, actually! I've been using Apple Pay for a while now. It's so convenient. I just **tap** my phone at checkout, and that's it. I don't even have to **take out** my wallet anymore.

Anna: That sounds really easy! I've been thinking about **signing up** for something like that, but I'm not sure if it's safe. I've heard people say it's risky to **link up** your bank account to an app like that.

Mark: I get that. But honestly, I think it's safer than carrying cash. Most apps **back up** your information with a password or fingerprint, so it's harder to **get hacked**. Plus, I can track all my spending in the app, which helps me **keep an eye on** my finances.

Anna: True, I like the idea of being able to **track** my spending. I've also been hearing a lot about crypto. Have you ever **looked into** using cryptocurrency to make payments?

Mark: I've thought about it, but I haven't **jumped into** the whole crypto thing yet. It's still pretty new, and I'm not sure if I want to **risk** my money on something that can go up and down so quickly.

Anna: Yeah, I feel the same way. I'm also a bit cautious about using things like Venmo or PayPal. I know they're popular, but I'm just not sure how they **stack up** against traditional banking systems.

Mark: Well, Venmo is convenient for splitting bills or paying friends, but I still **rely on** my bank for bigger transactions. It's good to have a mix of payment methods, I guess. Some things **work out** better with one system, while others **make sense** with another.

Anna: That's a good point. I think I'll **stick with** my credit card for now but maybe try out a digital wallet for smaller purchases. I'll just need to **figure out** which one works best for me.

Mark: Sounds like a solid plan. Just remember, no matter what system you choose, you need to **stay on top of** your security. Never share your PIN or password with anyone.

Glossary

Stick with: To continue using or doing something, rather than changing it.
Tried out: To test or experiment with something for the first time.
Take out: To remove or pull something from a bag, pocket, or container.
Signing up: To register for something, usually an account or service.
Link up: To connect two things, often electronically or online.

Back up: To support or protect something, often in terms of data.
Get hacked: To have one's account or information stolen by a hacker.
Keep an eye on: To monitor or watch something carefully.
Track: To follow or monitor progress, spending, etc.
Look into: To investigate or research something.
Jumped into: To begin or get involved in something quickly, often without hesitation.
Risk: To expose oneself to the possibility of loss or harm.
Stack up: To compare or measure how something is in relation to something else.
Rely on: To depend on something for support or success.
Work out: To turn out or result in a certain way.
Make sense: To be reasonable or understandable.
Stay on top of: To be in control of something or manage it well.
Figure out: To understand or solve something.

Speaking time

What payment methods do you usually use for online purchases? Why?
Do you think digital wallets and cryptocurrencies will **replace** traditional banking in the future? Why or why not?

Living on Low Wages

Sophie: Hey, Tom, how's everything going? How's work?

Tom: Ugh, honestly, it's been tough. I've been **getting by** on a pretty low salary lately. It's hard to **make ends meet** when your paycheck barely covers the bills.

Sophie: I can imagine. That sounds really stressful. It's hard to **stretch** every dollar when you're not making much. How are you managing?

Tom: Well, I've had to **cut back** on a lot of things. I don't go out much anymore, and I've been **holding off** on buying anything unnecessary. I just try to focus on what's really important, like rent and groceries.

Sophie: That's tough. Have you thought about **looking into** another job? Maybe something with better pay?

Tom: I've thought about it, but with my schedule, it's hard to **fit in** extra hours. And I've been trying to **stick with** this job since I've been here for a while. I don't want to **give up** just yet, but sometimes it feels like I'm not getting anywhere.

Sophie: I totally get that. It's hard to stay motivated when you're not seeing much progress. Have you been able to **save up** anything, or is it all going to bills?

Tom: Not really. I've been trying to **set aside** a little bit each month, but it's barely anything. If I **get lucky**, I might have enough for a small emergency fund, but that's about it.

Sophie: Yeah, I know how that feels. It's like you're constantly **playing catch-up**. Have you thought about trying to **cut down on** your expenses even more? Maybe there's something else you could adjust.

Tom: I've already cut out a lot, but maybe I could **look into** switching to cheaper services, like my phone plan or groceries. It's just tough when everything seems to **add up** so quickly.

Sophie: I hear you. It's not easy living on low wages. But hey, at least you're **getting by**, and sometimes that's all you can do. Hopefully, things will **pick up** soon.

Tom: I hope so. In the meantime, I'm just going to **keep pushing through** and hope for a better opportunity down the road.

Glossary

Getting by: To manage with limited resources or money.

Make ends meet: To earn enough to cover expenses and necessities.

Stretch: To make something last longer or go further, especially when resources are limited.

Cut back: To reduce spending or consumption.

Holding off: To delay or postpone something.
Looking into: To investigate or explore an option or opportunity.
Fit in: To find time or space for something.
Stick with: To continue doing something or staying with something for a while.
Give up: To quit or stop trying.
Save up: To accumulate money over time for a specific purpose.
Set aside: To reserve or save something for a future purpose.
Get lucky: To have something fortunate happen by chance.
Playing catch-up: Trying to improve or match progress after falling behind.
Cut down on: To reduce the amount or frequency of something.
Look into: To research or investigate something.
Add up: To accumulate or increase in a way that is noticeable.
Pick up: To improve or get better.
Keep pushing through: To continue making an effort despite difficulties.

Speaking time

What are some ways people can **cut back** on their spending if they're living on low wages?
Do you think living on low wages can affect someone's mental health? Why or why not?

Ending Excessive Spending

Lily: Hey, Mark, I've been meaning to ask you something. I've noticed you've been **spending a lot** lately. Are you planning to **cut back** anytime soon?

Mark: Ugh, you're right. I've been **blowing money** left and right. Honestly, I didn't realize how much I was **splurging** on things I don't really need. I think it's time I **get a grip** on my finances.

Lily: Yeah, I hear you. It can be easy to **get carried away** sometimes. So, what's your plan? How are you going to **scale back** on all the extra spending?

Mark: Well, first I'm going to **make a budget** and **stick to it**. I'll definitely have to **cut out** some of the things I've been **splurging on**, like eating out so much and buying random gadgets. It's hard, but I know I need to **get control** over it.

Lily: That sounds like a good idea. I've also heard people talk about **putting aside** a certain amount of money each month. Maybe you could **set up** an automatic transfer to a savings account so you don't even have to think about it.
Mark: That's a great suggestion! I think I'll **try out** that method. Also, I want to **hold off** on buying anything until I've paid off some of my current debts. It's really important that I **get back on track** before I spend any more.
Lily: Absolutely. It's all about prioritizing. You don't want to **fall behind** on your bills while spending on non-essentials. Do you have a plan for cutting back on other things, like subscriptions or shopping?
Mark: Yeah, I need to **go through** all my subscriptions and cancel the ones I never use. I also plan to **shop around** more before making big purchases. I'll **keep track** of every dollar I spend, so I don't **overspend** on things I don't really need.
Lily: Sounds like you've got it figured out. It'll be tough at first, but I think you can totally **turn things around**. Just take it one step at a time.
Mark: Thanks, Lily. I really appreciate your advice. I'm going to **stick with** this plan and hopefully see some good results soon.

Glossary
Spending a lot: To use up a lot of money, especially on unnecessary things.
Cut back: To reduce or decrease spending.

Blowing money: Spending money carelessly or without thinking.
Splurging: Spending a lot of money on things that are not essential or necessary.
Get a grip: To take control of a situation, especially when things are getting out of hand.
Get carried away: To become overly enthusiastic or excited, often leading to doing something too much.
Scale back: To reduce or limit something.
Make a budget: To plan and organize how to spend and save money.
Stick to it: To follow a plan or decision without deviating from it.
Cut out: To stop doing or using something.
Get control: To take charge or manage a situation.
Put aside: To save something, often money, for future use.
Set up: To arrange or establish something, such as an automatic payment.
Try out: To test something or give something a go.
Hold off: To delay or postpone something.
Get back on track: To return to a normal or intended course after a setback.
Fall behind: To not keep up with a schedule or payment.
Go through: To examine or check something carefully.
Shop around: To look at different options before making a purchase.
Keep track: To monitor or record something carefully.

Overspend: To spend more money than planned or than is reasonable.
Turn things around: To improve a situation or change it for the better.
Stick with: To continue doing something, especially when it gets tough.

Speaking time
How can you **cut back** on your spending without affecting your quality of life?
Do you think it's difficult to **stick to** a budget? Why or why not?

Having Bad Credit

Sara: Hey Jake, I've been meaning to ask you, how's everything going with your credit situation? You mentioned last time you were having trouble **keeping up** with your payments.
Jake: Ugh, yeah. Honestly, I've really **fallen behind** on a couple of bills. It's been tough trying to **catch up**, and now my credit score has taken a serious hit. I didn't think it would be this hard to **get back on track**.
Sara: I totally get it. Once you **fall behind** like that, it can feel impossible to **get out of** the hole. Have you looked into ways to **improve** your credit, or are you just waiting for it to **work itself out**?

Jake: I've tried a few things, like **paying off** some smaller debts to **build up** my score again, but it's taking way longer than I thought. I've even considered **applying for** a secured credit card, but I'm not sure if it'll **help out** in the long run.

Sara: That's actually a smart idea. If you can **stick to** making small payments and **avoid overspending**, it could **boost** your score over time. Have you thought about talking to a financial advisor to help you **work out** a plan to **bring down** your debt faster?

Jake: Yeah, I've been thinking about it. I guess I need to **get serious about** paying off the credit cards. The high interest rates are really **draining me**. If I don't **get a handle on** this soon, I could end up **paying off** these debts for years.

Sara: I know it feels overwhelming, but the key is to **stay on top of** things. Don't let the balances **pile up**. You could also try **cutting back** on unnecessary expenses so you can **free up** more money to pay down the debt faster.

Jake: Yeah, I need to **take a step back** and reevaluate my spending habits. I can't keep **living on the edge** with all this debt hanging over me. It's time to **tighten up** my budget.

Sara: Exactly. The sooner you **take control of** your finances, the better. And don't feel bad; a lot of people **go through** tough times with credit. You just have to **stick with** it and keep pushing forward.

Jake: Thanks, Sara. I appreciate the advice. I'm definitely going to **take action** and **fix** this mess before it gets worse.

Glossary
Keeping up: To maintain the necessary pace or level of payments.
Fallen behind: To not meet deadlines or payment schedules.
Catch up: To make up for lost time or payments.
Get back on track: To return to a normal or intended course after a setback.
Work itself out: To resolve or improve on its own without direct intervention.
Paying off: To completely repay a debt.
Build up: To increase or accumulate over time.
Apply for: To formally request something, like a loan or credit card.
Help out: To assist or provide aid in a situation.
Stick to: To follow a plan or decision without deviation.
Avoid overspending: To be careful not to spend more money than planned.
Boost: To increase or improve something, like a credit score.
Work out: To come up with a solution or plan.
Bring down: To reduce the amount or level of something.
Get serious about: To start paying close attention and making important decisions.

Draining me: To consume or use up resources, especially money, in a negative way.
Get a handle on: To manage or gain control over something difficult.
Stay on top of: To consistently monitor or manage something to prevent problems.
Pile up: To accumulate or increase to a high level.
Cutting back: To reduce or limit spending or use of something.
Free up: To make something available or accessible, usually money.
Take a step back: To pause and reassess the situation from a different perspective.
Living on the edge: To live in a risky or unstable situation.
Tighten up: To make something more controlled or disciplined.
Take control of: To manage or assume responsibility for something.
Go through: To experience something, usually something difficult.
Stick with: To continue with something despite difficulties.
Take action: To take steps to solve a problem or make changes.
Fix: To correct or resolve an issue.

Speaking time
What steps can you take to **boost** your credit score if you have bad credit?
How can you **cut back** on unnecessary spending to improve your financial situation?

Talking to a Bank Teller

Laura: Hey, Jake, I need your help. I've been trying to **figure out** how to transfer money from my savings to my checking account, but I'm not sure how to **go about** it. Do you know what I need to do?

Jake: Oh, that's easy! You can just **go up to** the teller and ask them to **set up** a transfer. It's really quick. They'll **take care of** everything for you.

Laura: I thought I could do it online, but I've been having some issues with my account. Maybe I'll just **stop by** the bank today. It's been a while since I've **checked in** on my account.

Jake: Yeah, that's a good idea. Sometimes it's easier to **sort out** problems in person. When you're there, just **bring up** the issue with your account, and they'll be able to help you **straighten things out**.
Laura: Alright, I'll definitely **stop by**. But what if they ask me to **fill out** a bunch of forms? I hate paperwork!
Jake: No worries! It's usually pretty straightforward. Just **fill in** the basic info, and if they need anything else, they'll let you know. It shouldn't take long to **wrap up**.
Laura: I hope so. Last time, I was there for an hour just trying to **clear up** a charge I didn't recognize. It was such a hassle.
Jake: Ugh, that sounds frustrating. Hopefully, you won't **run into** any problems this time. Just **make sure to** bring your ID and any necessary documents, just in case.
Laura: Good point. Thanks for the advice, Jake! I feel better now about **dealing with** the bank.
Jake: No problem, Laura! You'll **get it done**, no sweat.

Glossary
Figure out: To understand or solve something.
Go about: To start or begin something (like a task).
Go up to: To approach someone, especially to speak to them.
Set up: To arrange or establish something.

Take care of: To handle or deal with something.
Stop by: To visit a place briefly.
Check in: To look into or review something, like an account or status.
Sort out: To resolve a problem or situation.
Bring up: To mention or introduce a topic.
Straighten things out: To fix or clarify a situation.
Fill out: To complete a form or document.
Fill in: To provide the necessary details on a form.
Wrap up: To finish something.
Clear up: To resolve or explain a misunderstanding.
Run into: To encounter, often unexpectedly.
Make sure to: To ensure that something is done.
Deal with: To handle or manage something.
Get it done: To complete a task or goal.

Speaking time

What are some of the steps you would take if you had to **sort out** an issue with your bank account?

How do you feel about **dealing with** problems at the bank? Would you prefer to do it in person or online?

Bargaining with the Store Owner

Maria: Hey, Jake, I saw this beautiful jacket at the store yesterday, but it's a bit out of my budget. Do you think I could **talk down** the price a little?

Jake: Oh, for sure! You can always **try to negotiate**. Sometimes they're willing to **come down** a bit, especially if they see you're serious about buying.

Maria: Really? I thought they wouldn't budge, but I guess it can't hurt to **ask for** a discount, right?

Jake: Absolutely! If they **turn you down**, just politely thank them and move on. But, if they're **feeling generous**, they might even **throw in** something extra, like free shipping or a small gift.

Maria: That would be awesome! I'll definitely **give it a try**. How do you usually **go about** bargaining?

Jake: I usually **start off** by saying something like, "I really like this, but it's a little more than I was planning to spend." Then, I wait to see if they **offer** a lower price or if they're willing to **make a deal**.

Maria: I like that approach. I could also **bring up** that I saw a similar jacket for cheaper at another store. Do you think that would help?

Jake: That's a smart move! You can always **bring that up** as leverage. Just don't be too pushy—if they're **not budging**, you can always **walk away** and see if they'll change their mind.

Maria: I like the idea of **walking away**. I'm sure if they want to make a sale, they'll **come after** me with a better offer.

Jake: Exactly! It works like a charm sometimes. You just need to **stay calm** and **keep your cool**. They want to make a sale, and you want a good price—so it's a win-win!

Maria: Thanks for all the tips, Jake. I'll definitely **give it a shot** next time I'm at the store. Fingers crossed!

Jake: Good luck, Maria! I'm sure you'll **get a good deal**. Let me know how it goes!

Glossary

Talk down: To reduce the price or value of something through negotiation.

Try to: An expression used to suggest attempting something.

Come down: To lower the price or reduce an amount.

Ask for: To request something, usually as a favor or in a negotiation.

Turn you down: To refuse an offer or request.

Feeling generous: Willing to give or offer something, often for free or at a discount.

Throw in: To include something additional, often for free, in a deal.

Give it a try: To attempt or try something.

Go about: To approach or handle something in a particular way.

Start off: To begin something in a particular manner.

Offer: To present or propose something, usually as a deal.

Make a deal: To reach an agreement or negotiate a transaction.

Bring up: To mention or raise a topic during a conversation.
Not budging: Refusing to change a position or price.
Walk away: To leave a situation, often to show you're not desperate or to encourage further negotiation.
Come after: To pursue or attempt to engage someone again, usually after they've walked away.
Stay calm: To remain composed and not get upset.
Keep your cool: To maintain control over your emotions, especially in a stressful situation.
Give it a shot: To attempt or try something.
Get a good deal: To make a transaction where you feel you've paid a fair or favorable price.

Speaking time

When you want to **negotiate** for a better price, what are some good strategies to **start off** the conversation?

How do you feel about **walking away** during a negotiation if you're not getting the deal you want? Do you think it works?

Getting Your Pocket Picked

Emma: Ugh, you won't believe what happened to me this morning. I was at the market, just **minding my own business**, when I felt something strange. I looked down, and my wallet was gone!

Sophia: Oh no! You think you got **pickpocketed**?

Emma: Yeah, it must've been a pickpocket. I mean, I didn't even **see it coming**. One second I had my wallet, and the next, it was **gone without a trace**. I was so careful too!

Sophia: That's the thing with pickpockets. They're so good at what they do; they can **take your stuff** and you won't even notice. Did you **notice anyone suspicious** before it happened?

Emma: Actually, now that you mention it, there was a guy who seemed to be **hanging around** a little too close. I thought it was weird, but I didn't **think much of it** at the time.

Sophia: Yeah, that's often how they operate. They'll **get in close**, and you won't even realize what's going on until it's too late. Did you **report it** to anyone?

Emma: I did. I went straight to the police station and **filled out** a report. But honestly, I don't know if there's much they can do. I think they'll just **keep an eye out**, but it's not like they can track down the guy, right?

Sophia: It's probably tough to **catch a pickpocket**, especially when they're long gone by the time you realize what happened. But at least you **made sure** you reported it. Hopefully, they'll **pick up on** something if it's a known thief.
Emma: I hope so. I'm just really upset. I had some important cards in there too. I had to **call up** my bank and **cancel** everything. What a nightmare.
Sophia: Yeah, I can't even imagine. I always try to **keep an eye on** my bag when I'm out in crowded places. But sometimes it's hard to be alert all the time.
Emma: You're right. I guess I was just **caught off guard**. It's just so frustrating. I'll have to be way more careful next time.
Sophia: Definitely. Maybe you should **get a money belt** or something to keep your valuables safe. That way, even if someone tries to **snatch** something, they won't have an easy time.
Emma: Good idea. I'll definitely have to **keep that in mind**. I just hope I don't run into that guy again.
Sophia: Hopefully, you'll **stay out of his way** next time. And you know, if you ever feel like something's off, don't be afraid to **trust your gut**. It's usually right.

Glossary
Minding my own business: To be focused on your own activities and not interfering with others.

Pickpocketed: To have something stolen from your pocket, typically without your knowledge.
See it coming: To anticipate something before it happens.
Gone without a trace: Disappeared completely, with no evidence of where it went.
Take your stuff: To steal your belongings.
Notice anyone suspicious: To observe someone who seems out of place or unusual in a particular situation.
Hanging around: Staying nearby or lingering in a place without a clear purpose.
Think much of it: To not consider something as important or significant at the time.
Get in close: To approach someone in a way that doesn't attract attention.
Report it: To inform authorities or someone in charge about an incident.
Filled out: To complete a form or report with necessary information.
Keep an eye out: To watch or be vigilant for something or someone.
Pick up on: To notice or become aware of something.
Call up: To contact someone, usually by phone.
Cancel: To deactivate or stop a service, often referring to cards or accounts.
Keep an eye on: To carefully observe something.
Caught off guard: To be surprised or unprepared for something.

Get a money belt: A special kind of belt designed to hold valuables safely, often worn under clothing.
Snatch: To grab something quickly, often without permission.
Keep that in mind: To remember something for future consideration.
Stay out of his way: To avoid encountering someone, especially if they are dangerous or trouble.
Trust your gut: To follow your intuition or instincts, especially in uncertain situations.

Speaking time
What would you do if you noticed someone **hanging around** you and feeling suspicious in a crowded place?
How do you usually **keep an eye on** your valuables when you're out in public?

Dealing With Debt

Jack: Hey, Sarah, I've been meaning to ask you for some advice. I've really **got myself into a tight spot** with debt lately, and it's starting to feel like I'm just **digging myself deeper**. Do you have any tips on how to handle it?

Sarah: Oh, I totally understand. It can be tough, especially when it feels like the bills just **keep piling up**. First off, you really need to **take a hard look at** your expenses and **figure out where you're spending too much**. It's easy to get caught up in small things that add up over time.

Jack: Yeah, that's true. I've been **splurging** a bit too much on unnecessary stuff, like eating out. But, I mean, how do I even **start tackling** all these bills?

Sarah: Well, one thing you could do is **focus on paying off** the high-interest debts first. Once you **knock those out**, it'll be easier to **take care of** the others. You could also **try to negotiate** with your creditors and **see if you can work out** a more manageable payment plan.

Jack: I've never really thought about **calling up** the credit card companies or anything like that. I just figured they'd want me to **pay up** right away.

Sarah: Actually, you'd be surprised. Most of them are willing to **work with you**, especially if you're honest and show you're trying to pay. Sometimes, they'll even **lower your interest rate** or give you some breathing room.

Jack: That's reassuring to hear. But what if I just can't **make ends meet** this month?

Sarah: If it's really bad, you could **look into** consolidation loans. Basically, you combine all your debts into one monthly payment, which can be a lot easier to manage. But be careful, because it might end up costing you more in the long run if the interest rate is high.

Jack: Hmm, I'll have to **look into** that. I really don't want to **fall behind** on anything, though. The last thing I want is for my credit score to **take a hit**.

Sarah: I hear you. It's definitely important to **stay on top of** things and **not let it get out of hand**. Just make sure you don't **miss any payments**, even if it's just the minimum. That'll **keep you from falling deeper** into debt.

Jack: Thanks, Sarah. I think I've got a game plan now. I just need to **stick with it** and keep focused.

Sarah: Exactly! And don't be too hard on yourself—it's a process. Just keep **chipping away at it**, and you'll get there. The key is not to **let it overwhelm you**.

Glossary
Got myself into a tight spot: To find oneself in a difficult or uncomfortable situation.
Digging myself deeper: Making a bad situation worse.
Keep piling up: Accumulating over time.
Take a hard look at: To examine something carefully.
Figure out where you're spending too much: To identify areas where you're overspending.
Splurging: Spending money on things you don't need, often extravagantly.
Start tackling: To begin addressing or working on a problem.
Focus on paying off: To prioritize paying off certain debts first.
Knock those out: To finish or clear something, usually referring to tasks or debts.
Take care of: To manage or handle something, often referring to responsibilities.
Try to negotiate: To attempt to reach an agreement, typically for better terms or conditions.
See if you can work out: To find a solution or arrangement that works for both parties.
Calling up: To contact someone by phone.
Pay up: To pay what is owed.
Work with you: To cooperate and find a solution.
Lower your interest rate: To reduce the percentage charged on a loan or debt.

Make ends meet: To manage one's finances so that income covers expenses.
Look into: To investigate or explore an option.
Fall behind: To not meet deadlines or payments on time.
Take a hit: To suffer damage or loss, often in terms of reputation, finances, or performance.
Stay on top of: To maintain control or manage something effectively.
Not let it get out of hand: To prevent something from becoming uncontrollable.
Miss any payments: To fail to make a scheduled payment on time.
Chipping away at it: To gradually make progress on a large task or problem.
Let it overwhelm you: To allow something to become too much to handle emotionally or mentally.

Speaking time

How would you handle a situation where you couldn't **make ends meet** for a month?
What are some ways to **stay on top of** your debt and **avoid falling behind**?

Negotiating Price

Tom: Hey, Sarah, I'm thinking about buying a new laptop, but the price is a little higher than I was expecting. Do you think it's possible to **talk down** the price, or should I just **pay up**?

Sarah: Well, Tom, it never hurts to **give it a shot** and **negotiate**. Sometimes, stores have a little wiggle room, especially if you're willing to **haggle** a bit.

Tom: You're right. I've always heard that you can **bargain down** the price in a lot of places. But I don't want to **push my luck** too much and offend the seller.

Sarah: I get that. But if you're polite and **bring up** reasons why you think the price should be lower, it can really work in your favor. Maybe you could also **throw in** the fact that you've seen better deals elsewhere. That could **tip the scales** in your favor.

Tom: Hmm, that's a good idea. I could also **ask for** a discount, especially if I'm buying a couple of things at once, right?

Sarah: Exactly. Some stores might even **throw in** a free accessory or an extended warranty if you **push for it**. It's all about showing them that you're serious but not too demanding.

Tom: I like the sound of that! I've heard people say they've been able to **get the price down** just by asking if there's a sale or promotion I don't know about. Do you think that would work?

Sarah: Oh, for sure. You never know if there's a discount hiding in the system. And sometimes, just **asking around** can get you a better deal than you thought. Don't be afraid to **call up** the store if you think they might offer a better price.

Tom: I'll keep that in mind. I guess it's all about knowing when to **hold out** for a better deal and when to just **give in**.

Sarah: Exactly. Sometimes, it's worth waiting for a sale or a better offer to come along, but if you can't wait, then **making the first move** and **taking the plunge** can get you a decent price too.

Tom: Thanks, Sarah! I'll definitely try these tips. Maybe I'll even **push for** a freebie while I'm at it!

Glossary

Talk down: To convince someone to lower the price of something.

Pay up: To pay the full amount owed.
Give it a shot: To try something.
Negotiate: To discuss the price in order to reach a mutually agreeable amount.
Haggle: To argue or discuss the price, typically to get a better deal.
Bargain down: To lower the price through negotiation.
Push my luck: To take a chance and risk going too far.
Bring up: To mention or introduce something during a conversation.
Throw in: To include something extra for no additional cost.
Tip the scales: To influence the situation to your advantage.
Ask for: To request something, in this case, a discount.
Push for it: To make a strong request for something, like a discount or special offer.
Get the price down: To reduce the price of an item.
Asking around: Inquiring or asking different people for information or offers.
Call up: To contact someone by phone to inquire about something.
Hold out: To wait for a better deal or offer.
Give in: To agree to something after initially resisting.
Making the first move: Taking the first step in initiating an action or negotiation.
Taking the plunge: To take a risk or make a decision to move forward with something.

Speaking time

What would you do if a store offered you a price that's too high for your budget? Would you **haggle** or **hold out** for a better deal?

How do you feel about **calling up** a store to **ask for** a discount or a better offer? Do you think it's worth it?

Paycheck Deductions

Emma: Hey, Jake! I just got my paycheck, and I'm kind of shocked by how much they **took out** for taxes and other deductions. Do you know if this is normal?

Jake: Oh yeah, I've been there. Sometimes it feels like the government just **takes away** too much. But yeah, taxes are usually the biggest chunk that gets **taken out**. Did you check for any other deductions like insurance or retirement?

Emma: Yeah, I did. They also **pulled out** some for my 401(k) and health insurance. I didn't realize how much it would add up. I guess I should have **looked over** my pay stub more carefully last time.

Jake: That happens. Some people don't even **pay attention to** those deductions until they see the final amount. But if you **set up** contributions to your retirement plan, it'll help you in the long run.
Emma: True. I'm just not sure if I can **afford** all these deductions right now. It feels like the more I make, the more they **take out**.
Jake: I know what you mean. Sometimes it's tough when your paycheck **comes in** a little lower than you expected. But if it helps you save for the future, it's worth it. You just need to **keep track of** all the deductions and plan accordingly.
Emma: That's a good point. I guess I just have to **make sure** I budget a little more carefully each month. It would also help if I could **cut back on** some unnecessary spending.
Jake: For sure. You could always **look into** other ways to save too, like maybe adjusting your tax withholding. That way, you could get more in your paycheck upfront instead of waiting for a refund later.
Emma: I never thought about that. Maybe I should **bring it up** with HR and see if there's anything I can do to **adjust** things. I just don't want to mess up my taxes.
Jake: Yeah, definitely **check with** HR first. They can usually walk you through the process. It's better to **get it right** than to end up with a surprise come tax season.
Emma: Thanks, Jake! I feel a little better knowing there are options. I'll **look into** it soon.

Glossary
Took out: To deduct money from a paycheck or account (often for taxes, insurance, etc.).
Taken away: To remove something, often referring to something subtracted from your paycheck.
Pulled out: Another way of saying something was deducted.
Looked over: To examine something carefully, in this case, the pay stub.
Pay attention to: To notice or be aware of something.
Set up: To arrange or establish something, like a payment plan or automatic deductions.
Afford: To have enough money for something.
Come in: Refers to receiving the paycheck or income.
Keep track of: To monitor or record something over time.
Make sure: To ensure something happens or is done correctly.
Cut back on: To reduce or limit spending.
Look into: To investigate or examine something more closely.
Bring it up: To mention or introduce a topic in conversation.
Adjust: To make changes to something, like tax withholding.
Check with: To consult or confirm something with a person or department.
Get it right: To do something correctly, often to avoid mistakes or problems.

Speaking time
How do you feel about paycheck deductions? Do you **pay attention to** them, or do you just **look over** your pay stub briefly?

If you wanted to **adjust** your tax withholding to get more money upfront, what steps would you take? Would you **check with** your HR department?

Reselling Products for Profit

Alice: Hey Mark, I've been thinking about getting into reselling products for a profit. Have you ever tried it?

Mark: Oh, definitely! It's actually how I **got started** in the side hustle game. You just have to **figure out** what's trending and find good deals. It's all about finding products that people want but can't easily get.

Alice: That's what I was thinking. I've seen some people **flip** things they buy in bulk for a much higher price. But I'm not sure where to **start**. Any advice?

Mark: First off, you need to **keep an eye on** sales, especially at discount stores or even thrift shops. Sometimes you can **pick up** items for a fraction of the price, and then **resell** them online or locally.

Alice: Ah, I see! So it's really about **finding the right deals**. Do you mostly **buy in bulk**, or do you just grab things as you find them?

Mark: Both. It depends. Sometimes I **stock up** on items if I know they're in high demand. But other times, I just **jump on** a good deal when I see it. The key is to **stay on top of** the market and **be quick to act** when you see an opportunity.

Alice: Sounds like timing is really important. How do you know when you're **charging the right price**? I don't want to **overprice** or **undervalue** my stuff.

Mark: That's definitely something you need to **work out** over time. I usually **do some research** and check how much similar items are going for. It's important to **price competitively** but also **leave room for profit**.

Alice: Got it! I guess it's all about **keeping track of** your costs and making sure the numbers add up. But how do you handle shipping and returns?

Mark: Shipping can be tricky. I always **factor in** the cost of shipping when I'm pricing things. And as for returns, you can **set up** a clear return policy so people know what to expect. But if you're **reselling** through online platforms, they usually have those details covered.

Alice: That makes sense. I think I'm going to **give it a shot** and see how it goes. Thanks for all the tips, Mark!

Mark: No problem! Just **stick with it**, and you'll learn as you go. It can be a lot of work, but it's definitely worth it if you **play your cards right**.

Glossary
Got started: Began a new activity or business.
Figure out: To understand or solve something.
Flip: To buy something and sell it quickly for a profit.
Start: To begin something, such as a new venture or business.
Keep an eye on: To watch or monitor something carefully.
Pick up: To buy something, often at a lower price.
Resell: To sell something you have bought.
Buy in bulk: To purchase large quantities of an item at once.
Stock up: To accumulate goods in large quantities, usually for later use.
Jump on: To take advantage of an opportunity as soon as it arises.
Stay on top of: To stay informed and updated about something.
Be quick to act: To take action immediately when an opportunity presents itself.
Charging the right price: Setting a fair price for a product.
Overprice: To set a price that is too high for an item.
Undervalue: To set a price that is too low for an item.

Work out: To solve or figure something out.
Do some research: To investigate or gather information about something.
Price competitively: To set a price that is competitive with similar products.
Leave room for profit: To ensure that you make money by setting a price higher than your cost.
Keeping track of: Monitoring and managing something over time.
Factor in: To include something in your calculations.
Set up: To arrange or establish something, like a policy or system.
Give it a shot: To try something for the first time.
Stick with it: To continue doing something despite challenges.
Play your cards right: To make the right decisions and take the right actions to succeed.

Speaking time
If you were to start reselling products, what type of items would you **keep an eye on** to **pick up** and sell for a profit?
How would you **figure out** the right price for a product you're reselling without **undervaluing** it? What would be your strategy for **pricing competitively**?

Investing Your Money

John: Hey Sarah, I've been thinking about **putting my money to work**. You know, I've been saving for a while, and I want to start **investing**. Any tips?

Sarah: That's a great idea, John! Investing can really help you **build your wealth** over time. The first thing you need to do is **figure out** your goals. Are you thinking long-term, like for retirement, or are you looking to make some short-term gains?

John: I'm mostly looking at long-term growth. I want to **set myself up** for a comfortable retirement, but I don't know where to **start**. Should I just **jump in** with stocks, or is there something else I should look into?

Sarah: Well, stocks can definitely be a good option, but they can also be a bit risky. Have you thought about **diversifying** your investments? It's always a good idea to **spread out** your money in different areas—like real estate, bonds, and stocks. That way, if one investment doesn't **pan out**, you've got others to rely on.

John: Yeah, I've heard about that. I don't want to **put all my eggs in one basket**, so maybe I should **look into** some other options as well. What about mutual funds or ETFs? Are those worth considering?

Sarah: Absolutely! Mutual funds and ETFs are great for beginners because they let you **get in** on a variety of stocks or bonds without needing a lot of knowledge or research. It's also a way to **take some of the risk off your plate**, since they're more diversified than picking individual stocks.

John: That sounds pretty good. I've also heard people talk about **tracking** their investments. How do you **stay on top of** everything? Do you check your portfolio every day?

Sarah: I don't check it daily, but I do **keep an eye on** things, especially when there's market volatility. It's important not to **freak out** during market dips. Instead, you should **stick with** your strategy and **ride out** the ups and downs. Remember, investing is a marathon, not a sprint!

John: Good advice. I guess I shouldn't **get cold feet** just because of a little dip in the market, right?

Sarah: Exactly! A lot of new investors **get cold feet** when they see their investments drop, but it's all part of the process. Just **stay calm** and **trust the process**. Over time, your investments will likely grow.

John: I feel a lot more confident now. I'm going to **look into** some ETFs and maybe **spread my money around** in a few different areas. Thanks for the tips, Sarah!

Sarah: No problem! Just remember, the key is to **start early** and **stay consistent**. You'll be surprised at how much you can grow your money if you stick to it.

Glossary

Putting my money to work: Investing your money to generate income or profit.

Build your wealth: Accumulate money or assets over time.

Figure out: To determine or decide on something.

Set myself up: To prepare for future success or security.

Jump in: To begin something without hesitation.

Diversifying: Spreading your investments across different types of assets to reduce risk.

Spread out: To distribute or allocate resources in multiple areas.

Pan out: To work out as planned or expected.

Put all my eggs in one basket: To risk everything on one opportunity or investment.

Look into: To investigate or explore something further.

Get in: To participate in or enter an investment opportunity.
Take some of the risk off your plate: To reduce the risk you take on.
Stay on top of: To keep track of or remain informed about something.
Freak out: To become very anxious or upset.
Stick with: To remain committed to something.
Ride out: To endure or wait through a difficult situation.
Get cold feet: To become afraid or nervous about something.
Stay calm: To remain relaxed and not panic.
Trust the process: To have confidence that things will work out over time.
Start early: To begin something as soon as possible.
Stay consistent: To maintain a steady approach over time.

Speaking time

If you were to **start investing** your money today, what types of investments would you **look into** first and why?

How do you **stay on top of** your investments and **make sure** you're not **freaking out** during market fluctuations?

Having Cash Flow Problems

Emma: Hey, Mark, I've been having some **cash flow problems** lately. My business has been struggling to **bring in** enough money to cover expenses, and I'm starting to get worried. Have you ever dealt with something like this?

Mark: Oh, I know the feeling, Emma. It's tough when your expenses **outpace** your income. When I ran into similar issues, I had to **take a hard look at** my spending and find ways to **cut back** on non-essential stuff.

Emma: That's what I've been trying to do. I've already started **cutting down** on unnecessary expenses, but it still doesn't feel like enough. I've even tried to **reach out to** some clients to get paid earlier, but nothing's really working.

Mark: Sometimes, it's all about **finding new ways to bring in money**. Have you thought about **looking into** new revenue streams or even **restructuring** your pricing? It might help **bring in** more cash flow in the short term.

Emma: Yeah, I've considered it, but I don't know where to **start**. I don't want to **screw up** the relationships I have with my current clients. Have you ever tried **getting a loan** to help with cash flow?

Mark: I did, actually. I decided to **take out** a small business loan to **keep things going** when I was in a similar situation. It helped me **stay afloat**, but you have to be really careful with loans. The last thing you want is to **dig yourself into a deeper hole**.

Emma: That's exactly what I'm worried about. I don't want to **pile on** more debt. Maybe I should just **tough it out** a little longer and see if things **pick up**.

Mark: I get it. You don't want to rush into any big decisions. But if things don't **get better soon**, maybe you should **look into** other financing options like lines of credit or factoring. There are ways to **free up cash** without getting stuck with a huge loan.

Emma: I'll definitely **keep that in mind**. I just feel like I'm always **chasing my tail** with this. It's so stressful.

Mark: I hear you. But don't worry, you'll **pull through** this. Just keep focusing on what you can control, and don't be afraid to **ask for help** when you need it.

Emma: Thanks, Mark. I really appreciate the advice. I'll try to **hang in there** and **figure things out**. Hopefully, things will **turn around** soon.

Glossary
Cash flow problems: Issues with having enough money to cover expenses.
Bring in: To generate or earn.
Outpace: To surpass or exceed.
Take a hard look at: To carefully examine or evaluate.
Cut back: To reduce or decrease.
Reach out to: To contact or get in touch with.
Finding new ways to bring in money: Exploring different methods to generate income.
Looking into: To investigate or explore.
Restructuring: Changing the organization or structure of something, like prices or payment plans.
Screw up: To make a mistake or cause problems.
Getting a loan: Borrowing money from a financial institution.
Take out: To borrow or obtain something, often money.
Keep things going: To maintain or continue operations.
Stay afloat: To survive or manage through difficult times.
Dig yourself into a deeper hole: To make a bad situation worse.

Pile on: To add more to something, especially problems.
Tough it out: To endure or manage through a difficult situation.
Pick up: To improve or get better.
Look into: To research or consider.
Free up cash: To make money available or liquid.
Keep that in mind: To remember or consider.
Chasing my tail: To be busy but not making progress.
Pull through: To overcome difficulties or survive a tough time.
Ask for help: To seek assistance.
Hang in there: To persist through a difficult time.
Figure things out: To solve or resolve problems.
Turn around: To improve or change for the better.

Speaking time

What are some strategies you can use to **bring in** extra money if you're experiencing cash flow problems?

When you have a difficult financial situation, how do you **stay afloat** without taking on too much debt?

Checking Accounts and Writing Checks

Lily: Hey, John, I need to **figure out** how to manage my checking account better. I keep **running out of** funds, and I'm not sure what I'm doing wrong.

John: Yeah, I know what you mean. I used to **struggle with** that too, but over time, I learned to **keep track of** my spending better. It's important to **stay on top of** your account balance, especially if you're **writing checks** frequently.

Lily: That's exactly it! I feel like I'm always **scrambling** to make sure I have enough money in my account before I **write a check**. I really don't want to **bounce any checks**. Have you ever had that happen?

John: Oh, yeah. I made that mistake a couple of times. It's a **huge hassle** when you **overdraw** your account and the bank charges you fees. Now, I always make sure to **check** my balance before I **write a check**.

Lily: I think that's what I'm missing. I **tend to forget** to check the balance when I'm **writing a check** for bills. I should probably **set up** some alerts on my phone to remind me.

John: That's a good idea. Another thing I've done is **link** my checking account to my savings account, just in case I need to **transfer** money quickly to avoid any issues. That way, I don't have to worry about **coming up short**.

Lily: That's smart! I haven't done that yet. I'm still a little hesitant to **mix** my savings and checking accounts, though. I guess I should **get over** that.

John: Yeah, it's pretty convenient. And if you're **writing checks** for things like rent or utilities, it can really **save you** from unexpected problems. If you're still unsure, maybe **talk to** your bank about it. They can **walk you through** the best options.

Lily: I'll definitely do that. I just want to make sure I'm not **getting caught off guard** when I need to **write a check** or pay bills. I hate the thought of **incurring fees** just because I didn't plan ahead.

John: I hear you. Planning ahead is the key. Just **stay on top of** your finances and **take the time** to **double-check** your balance every now and then. It'll make a world of difference!

Lily: Thanks for the tips, John. I'm going to try to **stay on top of** things and be more careful about **writing checks**. Hopefully, it'll **pay off** in the long run.

Glossary
Figure out: To understand or solve something.
Running out of: To have very little left of something, especially money.
Keep track of: To monitor or record something.
Stay on top of: To manage or control something efficiently.
Writing checks: The act of using a check to pay for goods or services.
Bounce any checks: To write a check without enough money in the bank, causing it to be rejected by the bank.

Struggle with: To have difficulty or problems with something.
Scrambling: To make a quick, disorganized effort to achieve something.
Overdraw: To take more money out of an account than is available.
Hassle: An inconvenience or difficult situation.
Check: To verify or look at something, often referring to a bank balance.
Set up: To establish or arrange something, like a system or alert.
Link: To connect two accounts or systems for ease of use.
Transfer: To move money from one account to another.
Coming up short: Not having enough money.
Mix: To combine things that are usually separate, like savings and checking accounts.
Get over: To overcome or stop being concerned about something.
Save you: To prevent a problem or inconvenience.
Talk to: To communicate with someone for advice or information.
Walk you through: To guide you through a process step-by-step.
Getting caught off guard: Being unprepared for something unexpected.
Incurring fees: To accumulate charges, especially unwanted or unnecessary ones.
Double-check: To check something again to ensure accuracy.

Pay off: To be worthwhile in the end.

Speaking time
How do you usually **stay on top of** your checking account and avoid any issues with **writing checks**?

Have you ever experienced any difficulties when **writing a check** or managing your checking account? How did you deal with it?

Wiring Money to Another Country

Sarah: Hey Mark, I need some advice. I have to **wire money** to my sister in Canada, but I've never done it before. Do you have any experience with that?

Mark: Oh, yeah, I've **sent money** internationally a few times. It's not too complicated once you **get the hang of** it. The first thing you'll need to do is **find out** the details of her bank account, like the account number and the SWIFT code.

Sarah: SWIFT code? What's that?

Mark: It's a unique code that identifies a specific bank. You'll need it to **send the money** to the right place. Make sure you **double-check** all the information before you go ahead with the transfer, because if anything is off, it could cause problems.

Sarah: Got it. So, do I need to **go into** the bank, or can I do it online?

Mark: You can totally **do it online**. Most banks have an option to **wire money** through their website or app. It's faster and more convenient. But, if you prefer, you can also **go to** the bank in person and **fill out** a form.

Sarah: Sounds easier online. What about the fees? Are they crazy expensive?

Mark: It depends on the bank, but usually, there's a fee for **sending money** abroad. You'll probably pay a flat fee plus a percentage of the amount. Some services might offer lower fees if you're **sending a larger amount**. Just make sure you **check out** the fees before you confirm everything.

Sarah: I'll definitely do that. What about the exchange rate? Will I get a good deal, or do I need to **watch out for** hidden fees?

Mark: That's a good question. The exchange rate can vary from day to day. If you're **sending money** to a country with a different currency, make sure to **ask about** the rate they're offering before you send it. Some services might **mark up** the exchange rate, which means you're paying more than you should.

Sarah: I'll make sure to **ask about** that. I've also heard people mention things like PayPal or other apps. Are those options any good?

Mark: Yeah, PayPal and apps like Venmo or Wise are really popular for international transfers. The advantage of using apps is that they often offer lower fees and **quick transfers**. But again, you'll want to **look into** the exchange rate and fees before committing.

Sarah: Thanks for all the tips! I feel a lot more confident about it now. I just need to **make sure** I have all the details right before I go ahead with the transfer.

Mark: No problem! Just **take your time** and **do your research**. That way, you'll avoid any surprises. Good luck with the transfer!

Glossary

Wire money: To transfer money electronically from one bank account to another, usually across borders.

Get the hang of: To learn how to do something well or become familiar with it.

Find out: To learn something, especially information.

Double-check: To check something again to make sure it's correct.

Go into: To physically visit a place, like a bank.

Do it online: To complete a task using the internet rather than in person.

Go to: To visit a place.

Fill out: To complete a form or document by writing information on it.

Check out: To examine or investigate something.

Sending money: The act of transferring money from one person to another, often via a bank or online service.

Watch out for: To be cautious or aware of something, especially potential problems.

Ask about: To inquire about something or request information.

Mark up: To increase the price of something, usually unfairly or without clear justification.

Look into: To investigate or examine something in more detail.

Take your time: To do something without rushing.

Do your research: To gather information and make informed decisions before acting.

Speaking time
Have you ever had to **wire money** to another country? How did you go about it?
What are some things you think are important to **check out** when **sending money** abroad?

Reducing Household Expenses

Emma: Hey, Dan! I've been looking at our monthly budget, and honestly, I think we need to **cut back** on some of our household expenses. Do you have any ideas?

Dan: Yeah, I've noticed that too. It's easy to **rack up** bills without realizing it. One thing I've been doing is **switching off** lights and appliances when we're not using them. Little things like that really add up.

Emma: That's a great point! I've also been trying to **cut down on** how often we eat out. It's way cheaper to **cook up** a quick meal at home. Have you thought about **shopping around** for groceries to get better deals?

Dan: Absolutely! I've started **buying in bulk** for things like rice and pasta. It's way cheaper, and we use it all the time. Plus, I've been **looking into** using coupons and checking out sales more often.

Emma: Oh, I've been meaning to **look into** that too. We could even **cut back on** our subscription services. I think we still pay for a few we barely use, like that movie streaming service.

Dan: Yeah, that's a good one. We should probably **cancel** some of those. Also, I've been thinking about **changing** our internet plan. We're paying for super fast speeds, but we never really need them.
Emma: That's true! We could definitely **scale down** the internet package. And what about our phone plans? I bet we could **switch** to a cheaper option.
Dan: That's actually a great idea. I think we should **compare** some phone plans and see if we can get a better deal. Oh, and we've also been **running up** our electricity bill with the AC. Maybe we could **invest in** some fans instead?
Emma: Definitely. And maybe we should also **start putting aside** some savings for unexpected costs. It's better to be prepared.
Dan: Yeah, you're right. If we can **tighten up** our spending now, we'll be in a much better spot in the long run.
Emma: Exactly. Let's **keep track of** everything and review it every month to make sure we're staying on target.
Dan: Sounds good! We've got this.

Glossary
Cut back: To reduce or decrease something, especially expenses.
Rack up: To accumulate or increase something, like bills or costs.
Switch off: To turn off electrical devices or appliances.

Cut down on: To reduce the amount of something.
Cook up: To prepare or make food.
Shopping around: To compare prices at different stores or locations before buying something.
Buy in bulk: To purchase large quantities of something, usually at a discount.
Look into: To investigate or research something in more detail.
Cut back on: To reduce or lower the use of something.
Cancel: To end a service or subscription.
Change: To switch or alter something, such as a plan or service.
Scale down: To reduce the size or level of something.
Switch: To change from one option to another.
Compare: To examine and evaluate two or more things to find the best choice.
Run up: To accumulate or increase, especially in terms of bills or debt.
Invest in: To spend money on something with the expectation of future benefits.
Start putting aside: To save money for a future need.
Tighten up: To become more careful or stricter, especially with spending.
Keep track of: To monitor or stay aware of something, such as finances.

Speaking time

What are some simple ways you can **cut back on** your household expenses?

Do you think **shopping around** for better deals on groceries and services is worth the time and effort? Why or why not?

Types of Bank Accounts

Alice: Hey, Tom, I've been thinking about opening a new bank account. I already have a checking account, but I'm not sure if I should **set up** a savings account too. What do you think?

Tom: I think a savings account could be a good idea, especially if you want to **put aside** some money for the future. But it depends on what your goals are. Are you looking to **build up** your savings, or just keep some extra cash handy for emergencies?

Alice: I'd like to **build up** my savings, but I also need something to manage my day-to-day spending. My checking account is just not cutting it. Maybe I should **switch** to a different one?

Tom: Well, if you want to have more flexibility, you might want to **look into** a high-yield savings account. You can earn more interest than a regular one. Also, there are **checking accounts** that offer rewards, like cashback for your purchases.

Alice: That sounds interesting. How does a high-yield savings account work? Do I have to **keep up** with minimum deposits or balances?

Tom: Yeah, usually, you have to **maintain** a minimum balance to earn the higher interest rate. But the good thing is that the money you **put in** grows faster. You should **ask around** to compare rates between different banks to find the best deal.

Alice: That makes sense. I might also need to **set up** an emergency fund. How about money market accounts? I've heard they're a good option.

Tom: Money market accounts can be great, but they usually require a higher minimum deposit. Still, they tend to offer better interest rates than a basic savings account. If you're okay with a higher initial investment, it could be worth it.

Alice: I see. I also want to be able to **pull out** money without any fees, but some accounts have restrictions, right?

Tom: Exactly. With some accounts, if you **take out** money too often, you could end up with a fee. It's a good idea to **check out** the fine print before you commit. Some accounts have a limited number of withdrawals each month without penalties.

Alice: That's helpful. I guess I need to **narrow down** my options and see which one fits my needs best.

Tom: Yep, and make sure to **keep track of** the fees too. They can add up if you're not careful. Do some research, and you'll find the right fit for you!

Alice: Thanks for all the advice, Tom! I'll definitely **look into** everything before making a decision.

Tom: No problem, happy to help. Good luck with your bank hunt!

Glossary

Set up: To establish or open something, such as a bank account.

Put aside: To save money or reserve something for future use.

Build up: To accumulate or grow something, like savings or a balance.

Switch: To change from one option to another.

Look into: To investigate or research something in more detail.

Keep up: To maintain a certain level or standard.

Maintain: To keep or continue something at a required level.

Ask around: To inquire with several people or sources to get more information.

Take out: To withdraw money from an account.

Check out: To examine or inspect something more closely.

Narrow down: To reduce or limit options to a few choices.

Keep track of: To monitor or stay aware of something, such as account balances or fees.

Speaking time
What type of bank account do you think is best for saving money in the long term, and why?
How do you usually decide which bank or financial institution to go with when opening a new account?

Marrying a Gold Digger

Jake: Man, I don't know what to think anymore. I've been **dating around**, and I met this girl who seems really interested in me, but something's off. It's like she's only after my money.
Tom: Oh no, Jake. Are you saying she might be a **gold digger**?
Jake: Yeah, I'm starting to **pick up on** the signs. Every time we go out, she's always asking about what I do for a living, how much money I make, and even where I live. It's like she's trying to **figure out** how much I'm worth.

Tom: That's a major red flag, my friend. I've heard a lot of stories about people getting **caught up in** relationships like that. A gold digger will try to **weasel in** on your wealth without giving much in return. You don't want to **fall into** that trap.

Jake: Exactly! But at the same time, I don't want to **jump to conclusions**. Maybe I'm overthinking it. She's really attractive, and we get along well. But I can't stop feeling like she's just **hanging around** to see what she can get from me.

Tom: It's tough, man. A lot of people get **swept up in** the excitement of a relationship and don't notice the warning signs until it's too late. You need to **watch out** for any signs that she's just in it for the money. Does she ever offer to **chip in** or help out with expenses when you go out?

Jake: Not really. She always seems to **let me pick up** the tab. And when I bring up doing something simple, like a cheap date night, she always has an excuse for why it's not a good idea. It's like she wants the luxury stuff without putting in any effort.

Tom: That's a huge clue right there. A genuine person will **step up** and contribute, or at least be willing to **meet you halfway**. But if she's only interested in what you can **bring to the table**, that's definitely a sign of a gold digger.

Jake: Yeah, I think you're right. I don't want to **get stuck** in a relationship where I'm just a paycheck to someone. It's like they're more focused on your bank account than your heart.

Tom: That's the thing, Jake. You've got to **be careful** not to let someone take advantage of you. It's about finding someone who's genuinely interested in you as a person, not just your wallet. You can always **fall back on** your instincts.

Jake: I hear you, man. I guess I'll **keep an eye out** and see how things unfold. I don't want to **rush into** anything, especially if there's a chance I'm dealing with a gold digger.

Tom: Definitely, take your time. You don't want to **get involved** in something that's going to be a headache down the road. Trust me, it's better to **back off** now than regret it later.

Glossary
Gold digger: A person who forms relationships primarily to obtain money or gifts from their partner.
Dating around: To go on dates with different people, not necessarily in a committed relationship.
Pick up on: To notice or become aware of something.
Figure out: To understand or solve something.
Caught up in: To become involved in something, often without realizing it.
Weasel in: To gain entry or influence in a way that is sneaky or underhanded.
Fall into: To unintentionally become involved in something, typically something negative.

Jump to conclusions: To make a judgment without enough evidence or information.
Hanging around: To stay close to someone with no specific purpose, possibly for personal gain.
Watch out: To be careful or cautious about something.
Chip in: To contribute money or effort to a shared cause.
Let me pick up: To pay for something (like dinner or a bill).
Step up: To take responsibility for something or to offer help.
Meet you halfway: To compromise or make an effort to accommodate someone else.
Bring to the table: To offer something of value, typically in a relationship or business context.
Get stuck: To become trapped in a situation that is hard to escape from.
Be careful: To proceed with caution.
Fall back on: To rely on something or someone in times of need.
Rush into: To make a decision or action too quickly without considering all aspects.
Get involved: To become part of a situation or relationship.
Back off: To withdraw or stop pursuing something.

Speaking time
Have you ever experienced a situation where you felt someone was more interested in your money than you? How did you handle it?

What qualities do you think are important in a relationship, and how can you tell if someone is truly interested in you as a person?

Using Coupons and Rebates

Sarah: Hey, Jack! I just came back from shopping, and I saved a ton of money today using coupons. Have you ever **used coupons** before?

Jack: Oh, absolutely. I've been **stocking up** on them lately. It's crazy how much you can **save up** if you know where to look. Did you find anything good?

Sarah: Yeah, I got a great deal on my groceries. I always **check out** those coupon websites and see if there are any discounts for things I actually need. You wouldn't believe how much you can **cut down on** your expenses just by doing that.

Jack: That's true! I've been meaning to **look into** some rebates for my electronics purchases. I heard they can really help **bring down** the price of big-ticket items. Have you ever used those?

Sarah: Oh yeah, I've **gotten back** a few bucks on rebates in the past. It's a bit of a hassle sometimes, but it's totally worth it if you can **cash in on** those deals. You just have to remember to **send in** all the required documents on time.

Jack: That's the trick, right? I always forget to **follow through** on those rebate offers, but the ones I've actually done have saved me a nice amount. You just have to **keep track of** all the dates and stuff.

Sarah: Exactly. But even when I forget to **send off** the rebate forms, I still love using coupons at the store. It's fun to **watch the total drop** when they scan them. I feel like I'm getting away with something!

Jack: Haha, I know that feeling! It's like **getting a steal** every time you walk out of the store. And if you **stack up** coupons—using more than one for the same item—you really get the most out of your purchases.

Sarah: Yeah, I try to **combine** the coupons with sales to get the best deal. It can be a little tricky, but if you're patient, you can **take advantage of** some great savings.

Jack: I think I need to **step up** my coupon game. I always feel like I'm missing out when I see other people **racking up** all those savings.

Sarah: It's definitely worth the effort. You just have to **get into** the habit of looking for them, and before you know it, you'll be saving all over the place. Plus, the more you **clip**, the more you'll get used to finding the best deals.

Jack: Alright, I'm going to **give it a try** this weekend. Maybe I'll start by **checking out** some online deals and see what I can **stock up on**.

Glossary

Used coupons: To take advantage of discounts offered through couponing.

Stocking up: Collecting or gathering items in advance, often to save money.

Save up: To accumulate money over time to use later.

Check out: To examine or explore something, usually for a potential purchase.

Cut down on: To reduce the amount of something.

Look into: To investigate or research something.

Bring down: To lower the price of something.

Gotten back: To receive a refund or rebate after making a purchase.

Cash in on: To take advantage of an opportunity to make money or save money.
Send in: To submit or mail something (like forms or documents).
Follow through: To complete or finish something, especially after starting it.
Keep track of: To monitor or stay updated on something.
Send off: To mail or submit something, typically an application or form.
Watch the total drop: To see the total cost decrease after using discounts.
Getting a steal: Getting something at a very low price or good deal.
Stack up: To combine multiple items or offers to maximize savings.
Combine: To join two or more things together for better value.
Take advantage of: To use something for one's benefit.
Step up: To improve or increase one's efforts.
Racking up: Accumulating a large amount of something, usually savings.
Get into: To start becoming involved or interested in something.
Clip: To cut out or save coupons from newspapers or magazines.
Give it a try: To attempt or try something new.

Speaking time

How do you usually save money when you shop? Do you prefer using coupons or rebates?

What is one item you would love to get a great deal on, and how would you go about finding a discount or coupon for it?

Being in Debt

John: Hey, Alex, I've been meaning to ask you—how do you manage being **in debt**? I'm seriously struggling with mine lately. I just can't seem to **catch up**.

Alex: Oh man, I totally get it. It can be overwhelming. When I was **drowning in debt**, I felt like there was no way out. But I decided to **take control** of my finances and start paying things off bit by bit.

John: That sounds like good advice, but every time I think I'm getting ahead, something else comes up. It's like the bills just **keep piling up**.

Alex: I know that feeling! It's tough, but the key is to **stay on top of** it. I started by **setting aside** a portion of my paycheck each month and **putting it toward** my debts. Even if it's not a lot, it adds up over time.

John: I've tried doing that, but it feels like the interest rates are just **eating away at** my money. It's hard to make any progress when I'm constantly **paying off** just the interest.

Alex: Trust me, I've been there too. What really helped me was looking into **consolidating** my debt. I found a lower-interest loan to **pay off** my credit cards, which made it easier to keep track of everything.

John: That sounds interesting. But I'm afraid it's going to **set me back** even more if I don't do it right. How do I even **get started** with something like that?

Alex: First things first, you need to **figure out** exactly how much you owe and where it's going. Once you know the total amount, you can **shop around** for a good consolidation loan with a lower interest rate. It's all about **finding the best deal**.

John: Okay, so I shouldn't just **jump into** any loan offer that comes my way. I'll need to **weigh my options** carefully.

Alex: Exactly! It's all about making sure that you **stay within** your budget and don't **dig yourself deeper** into debt. Trust me, once you get on the right track, it will feel like a weight is **lifting off** your shoulders.

John: Thanks, Alex. I'm definitely going to **look into** consolidation. I just hope I can **stay focused** and get my finances back on track.

Glossary
In debt: Owing money to someone or a financial institution.
Catch up: To reach the point where you are no longer behind, especially in terms of payments.
Drowning in debt: Feeling overwhelmed or unable to manage debt.
Take control: To begin managing something in a way that gives you authority or responsibility.
Keep piling up: To keep increasing or accumulating over time.
Stay on top of: To manage something effectively without letting it get out of hand.
Setting aside: To reserve or save a portion of something for a specific purpose.

Putting it toward: Using money or resources for a specific goal or payment.
Eating away at: Gradually reducing or depleting something, often in an undesirable way.
Paying off: To pay the full amount of a debt.
Consolidating: Combining several debts into a single debt, usually at a lower interest rate.
Set me back: To delay progress or cost more than expected.
Get started: To begin taking action or making progress toward something.
Figure out: To understand or solve something.
Shop around: To look at different options or prices before making a decision.
Finding the best deal: Searching for the most advantageous offer or opportunity.
Jump into: To start something without careful consideration or planning.
Weigh my options: To consider all available choices before making a decision.
Stay within: To remain inside certain limits, such as a budget.
Dig yourself deeper: To get into a worse situation or make things more difficult for yourself.
Lifting off: To feel relieved or free from a burden.

Speaking time
What strategies do you think could help you reduce your debt?

Have you ever considered consolidating your debt? Why or why not?

Accepting Credit Cards as a Payment Option

Sarah: Hey, Mike! I've been thinking about **upgrading** the payment options for my business. Right now, I only accept cash, but I'm starting to wonder if I should **set up** credit card payments too. What do you think?

Mike: Oh, for sure! I think accepting credit cards is a game-changer. It'll help **bring in** more customers who prefer to pay that way. It's so convenient for people, especially when they don't have cash on hand.

Sarah: Yeah, I get that. The thing is, I'm not sure how to **go about** setting it up. Do I need to **get in touch with** the bank, or is it more complicated than that?

Mike: It's actually pretty straightforward. You just need to **sign up** with a payment processor like Square or PayPal. They'll **set you up** with everything you need, like a point-of-sale system and a way to **process** the payments. It doesn't take long at all.

Sarah: That sounds easy enough. But I'm worried about the fees. I've heard some companies **charge** a lot for each transaction. Is that true?

Mike: Yeah, some companies **take a cut** of every payment you process, but it's usually a small percentage. You'll need to **factor in** those fees when you're pricing your products. But overall, it'll be worth it because you'll be **bringing in** more business.

Sarah: Good point. I guess I'll just have to **raise** my prices a bit to **cover** those extra fees. How do you handle returns or chargebacks though? That part sounds tricky.

Mike: It can be, but you just have to **stay on top of** your transactions. Most payment processors offer tools to **deal with** returns and disputes. You'll need to keep records of your sales, but if you're on top of it, it won't be a problem.

Sarah: Thanks, Mike. I feel a lot better about **moving forward** with this now. I think I'm ready to **take the plunge** and start accepting credit cards.

Mike: You'll do great! It's really one of the best decisions I've made for my business. Let me know if you need help **setting up** your system—I'm happy to **help out**.

Glossary

Upgrading: Improving or enhancing something, such as a system or service.

Set up: To establish or arrange something, such as a payment system.

Bring in: To attract or generate, especially business or customers.

Go about: To begin or approach doing something.

Get in touch with: To contact or reach out to someone.
Sign up: To register for a service or program.
Set you up: To provide or arrange for necessary tools or systems.
Process: To handle or complete a transaction or payment.
Charge: To ask for money for a service or product.
Take a cut: To take a portion of the total amount, usually as a fee.
Factor in: To consider or include something in a decision or calculation.
Raise: To increase or make higher, such as prices or fees.
Cover: To pay for or compensate for something.
Stay on top of: To manage or keep control of something efficiently.
Deal with: To handle or address a situation or problem.
Moving forward: Making progress or continuing with something.
Take the plunge: To make a bold decision or commitment to something.
Help out: To assist or provide help to someone.

Speaking time

What are the benefits of accepting credit cards for your business?

What challenges do you think could arise from accepting credit cards, and how could you handle them?

Problem with a Restaurant Check

Sarah: Hey, Mike! You won't believe what happened to me at lunch today. I was at that new restaurant down the street, and when I went to **pay the check**, they charged me twice for the same dish!

Mike: Oh no! That's frustrating. Did you **point out** the mistake to them right away?

Sarah: Yeah, I did. I **brought it up** with the waiter, and he seemed a little confused at first. But then he went back to the kitchen to **check it out**, and sure enough, they had **charged** me for two orders of the same pasta.

Mike: Good thing you caught that! What did they do to fix it?

Sarah: They were pretty good about it. The manager came over, **apologized** for the mix-up, and promised to **take care of** it. He even offered me a free dessert for the inconvenience!

Mike: Wow, that's a nice way to **make up for** the mistake. Did they **take off** the extra charge from the bill?

Sarah: Yep! They **removed** the extra charge, and I ended up paying the correct amount. But it's still kind of annoying when something like that happens, you know?
Mike: I totally get it. It can really **throw you off** when there's an error with your bill. But at least they **fixed it** quickly. It sounds like they were trying to **make things right**.
Sarah: Yeah, I appreciate that they handled it well. It just took me a while to **get over** the fact that I almost paid double. But it's all good now!
Mike: At least you didn't have to **fight** to get the extra charge removed. A lot of places can be difficult about that kind of thing. It sounds like they really **care about** keeping customers happy.

Glossary
Pay the check: To settle the bill after a meal at a restaurant.
Point out: To bring attention to something or highlight an issue.
Bring it up: To raise or mention a topic or problem.
Check it out: To investigate or look into something.
Charge: To bill someone for an item or service.
Take care of: To resolve or handle a situation.
Make up for: To compensate for a mistake or problem.
Take off: To remove or deduct something from a bill.

Removed: Taken away or subtracted.
Throw you off: To cause confusion or disrupt your normal expectations.
Fix it: To correct a mistake or problem.
Make things right: To resolve a problem or compensate for an issue.
Get over: To stop being upset or affected by something.
Fight: To argue or struggle for something.
Care about: To be concerned with or value something.

Speaking time
How would you handle a situation where you're charged incorrectly at a restaurant?
Why do you think it's important for restaurants to address billing mistakes quickly?

A Mistake in a Hotel Bill

Alice: Hey, Jake! I just checked out of the hotel, and there's a huge mistake on my bill. They **charged me** for an extra night I didn't stay!

Jake: Oh, that's the worst! Did you **bring it up** to the front desk?

Alice: Yeah, I did. I immediately **pointed it out** to the receptionist. She was a bit surprised, but then she said she'd **look into** it and **check** the system.

Jake: Hopefully they'll **sort it out** quickly. Did they seem like they were going to **fix it**?

Alice: She said they would **get back to me** in a few minutes, but I had to **wait around** for a while. I was a little worried they might **try to brush it off**.

Jake: I can't stand it when they **do that**. So, what happened? Did they **take care of** the mistake?

Alice: Eventually, they **came back** to me and said it was just a **glitch** in their system. They **adjusted** the charge and **took off** the extra night from my bill.
Jake: Glad to hear they **fixed it**. It's always better when they **own up to** their mistake. I'm guessing you didn't have to **argue** much?
Alice: Nope, luckily, they were really polite about it. I'm just glad it's all **settled** now.
Jake: Yeah, me too. It's such a hassle when things like that happen, but it's good that they **didn't give you a hard time**. At least everything worked out in the end.

Glossary
Charge: To bill someone for something.
Bring it up: To mention or raise an issue or topic.
Point out: To highlight or draw attention to something.
Look into: To investigate or check something carefully.
Check: To verify or confirm something, often used in the context of reviewing information.
Sort it out: To resolve or solve a problem.
Fix it: To correct or resolve a problem.
Get back to me: To return with an answer or solution after some time.
Wait around: To stay in one place while waiting for something to happen.
Brush it off: To ignore or dismiss something.
Take care of: To handle or resolve an issue.
Come back: To return with a response or solution.

Glitch: A minor, often temporary problem or malfunction.
Adjust: To change or correct something, often in a small way.
Take off: To remove or subtract something (from a bill, for example).
Own up to: To admit or take responsibility for something.
Argue: To engage in a disagreement or discussion, often to resolve a problem.
Settle: To resolve or bring a matter to a conclusion.
Give you a hard time: To be difficult or uncooperative.

Speaking time
How would you handle a situation where there's a mistake on your hotel bill?
Why is it important for a hotel to resolve billing errors quickly and efficiently?

Making a Bet

Tom: Hey, Sarah! I just **made a bet** with Mike that I could beat him at pool tonight. He's pretty confident, but I think I've got this.
Sarah: Oh, wow! You're **taking him on**? I didn't know you were so good at pool.
Tom: Yeah, I've been practicing a bit. But honestly, I'm not sure if I can actually **pull it off**. Mike's been playing for years.
Sarah: Well, it sounds like a fun challenge. What's the **wager**? What do you get if you win?
Tom: If I win, he has to buy dinner for a week. But if he wins, I've gotta **take him out** for a night on the town.
Sarah: That's a pretty good deal! Do you think you can **come through** with a win?

Tom: I'm not sure. I'm just trying to **keep my cool**. I know I have the skills, but Mike's tricky.
Sarah: Well, it's all about **playing it smart**. Don't let him **talk you into** something you don't want to do, though.
Tom: Oh, trust me. I'm ready. If I win, I'll make sure to **rub it in** a little bit, haha.
Sarah: Well, good luck! Just don't **get carried away** with all that confidence. Remember, anything can happen in a game like that.
Tom: True! I'll keep my fingers crossed, though. I've got a good feeling about this.

Glossary

Made a bet: To agree on a wager or challenge.
Taking him on: Challenging or competing against someone.
Pull it off: To succeed or accomplish something difficult.
Wager: A bet or the terms of a betting agreement.
Take him out: To go somewhere with someone, usually to a restaurant or event.
Come through: To deliver or succeed in a challenge or promise.
Keep my cool: To remain calm and not get overly stressed or excited.
Playing it smart: To make wise or careful decisions.
Talk you into: To convince someone to do something.
Rub it in: To remind someone of a win in a boastful or teasing way.

Get carried away: To become overly enthusiastic or emotional about something.
Keep my fingers crossed: To hope for good luck or a positive outcome.

Speaking time
Have you ever made a bet with someone? What was it about?
What do you think makes a bet more exciting—high stakes or the challenge of competing?

Black Friday

Mark: Hey, Jamie! Are you planning to **go all out** this year for Black Friday?
Jamie: Oh, for sure! I've already **set aside** some cash for the sales. I've been **waiting for** this all year. Are you?
Mark: Definitely. I'm going to **hit up** a few stores early. I heard the deals this year are supposed to be crazy.
Jamie: I'm not sure if I want to **brave the crowds**, though. Last year was insane. People were **pushing and shoving** just to grab a TV.

Mark: I totally get it. But I'm planning to **get in on** some good discounts, especially on electronics. It's really the only time of year you can **pick up** a nice gadget for cheap.
Jamie: True, true. I've been meaning to **stock up on** some stuff for the house. Plus, I need to **replace** my old laptop. It's starting to **give out** on me.
Mark: Yeah, I'm going to **check out** some laptops too. Maybe I'll **snag** a good deal before they're all gone. You know how it is, right?
Jamie: Oh, definitely. You have to **jump on** the good deals fast or they'll be sold out. The best stuff always **sells out** in minutes.
Mark: I know, right? It's like you have to **be on the lookout** all day. But hey, it's all worth it for the savings.
Jamie: For sure. I'll **stop by** a few stores, then maybe I'll just **order online** for the rest. I don't think I can deal with the madness in person.
Mark: Sounds like a plan. Just don't **get too caught up** in the shopping frenzy. It's easy to **spend more than you planned** if you're not careful.
Jamie: Good advice! I'll try not to **go overboard**. I just want to **pick up** a few good deals without losing my mind.

Glossary
Go all out: To spend a lot of money or effort on something.
Set aside: To save or keep something for a specific purpose.

Waiting for: Anticipating or looking forward to something.
Hit up: To visit or go to a place, typically a store.
Brave the crowds: To deal with large, chaotic crowds of people.
Pushing and shoving: Physical movements to get through a crowd or situation.
Get in on: To participate in something, like a sale or deal.
Pick up: To buy or obtain something.
Stock up on: To gather or accumulate supplies or items in large amounts.
Replace: To get something new to substitute for an old or broken one.
Give out: To stop working or functioning properly.
Check out: To look at or investigate something.
Snag: To grab or obtain something quickly, usually at a good price.
Jump on: To take advantage of an opportunity quickly.
Sells out: When a product or item is completely bought and no longer available.
Be on the lookout: To watch carefully or keep an eye out for something.
Stop by: To visit briefly.
Order online: To buy products through the internet.
Get too caught up: To become overly involved in something, often to the detriment of one's plans.

Spend more than you planned: To exceed your budget or intended expenditure.
Go overboard: To do something to an excessive degree.

Speaking time
Have you ever gone shopping on Black Friday? What was your experience like?
Do you prefer shopping in stores on Black Friday, or do you like shopping online for the deals? Why?

File Tax Return

Sarah: Hey, Chris, have you started to **fill out** your tax return yet?
Chris: Not yet. I've been putting it off because I'm worried I'll **mess up** the forms. I'm not exactly a tax expert!

Sarah: I get that! I always **dread** doing mine. But you really should **get on** it soon—April 15th is just around the corner.

Chris: I know! I was actually thinking about **hiring** a tax professional to help me **sort through** all the paperwork. I just don't want to **miss out** on any deductions.

Sarah: That's a smart move. I've done my taxes myself for years, but I always **double-check** everything before I **submit** it online. I don't want the IRS to come after me!

Chris: Yeah, I've heard they can **crack down** hard if you make a mistake. So, do you **use** one of those online tools like TurboTax?

Sarah: Yep, I usually **file** it myself with TurboTax. It **walks you through** the whole thing and even **suggests** deductions based on your expenses. But I always **look over** everything before I click "submit."

Chris: That sounds easy enough. Maybe I'll **give it a try** this year. How long does it take to **get back** your refund?

Sarah: It usually takes about two weeks, but if you **file** electronically and have direct deposit, it can be quicker.

Chris: Good to know. I think I'll try to **wrap up** my return this weekend so I'm not stressing at the last minute.

Sarah: Smart choice. The sooner you **get it done**, the sooner you'll get your refund!

Glossary
Fill out: To complete a form or document.

Mess up: To make a mistake or do something incorrectly.
Get on: To begin or start doing something.
Dread: To feel anxious or worried about something.
Hire: To employ someone for a specific task or job.
Sort through: To organize or look through something carefully.
Miss out: To fail to take advantage of something.
Double-check: To verify or check something again to ensure accuracy.
Submit: To officially send in something, like a form or application.
Crack down: To take strong or strict action against something.
Use: To make use of a tool, system, or service.
File: To officially submit or register a form or document.
Walk through: To explain or guide someone through a process.
Suggest: To offer a recommendation or idea.
Look over: To review or examine something carefully.
Give it a try: To attempt or try something new.
Get back: To receive something after sending or waiting for it (e.g., a refund).
Wrap up: To finish or complete something.
Get it done: To finish a task or project.

Speaking time

How do you feel about filing your taxes—do you find it stressful or easy? Why?

Have you ever hired a professional to help with your taxes? Would you recommend it? Why or why not?

Tax Refund

Jack: Hey, Emily! Did you **file** your taxes yet? You know, tax season is almost over!

Emily: Yeah, I did. I actually **submitted** everything last week. I can't wait to see if I'll **get back** a refund this year. It would really **help out** with some of my bills.

Jack: I totally hear you. I always **look forward to** my tax refund. It feels like free money. Do you think you'll **get a good amount** back?

Emily: I'm hoping so! I've had some pretty big medical expenses this year, so I'm crossing my fingers that I'll **get something back** for that. I've been saving my receipts, so I'm pretty sure I'll qualify for a deduction.

Jack: That sounds like a smart move. I usually **get by** just with the standard deduction, but I've heard those medical deductions can really **add up**.

Emily: Exactly! I'm also hoping my student loan interest counts for something. Honestly, I just want to **break even** this year. If I get too much back, I'll probably just **spend** it on more debt.

Jack: Yeah, I get it. I like to use my refund to **pay off** a chunk of my credit card bills. It feels good to **knock out** some debt with that extra cash.

Emily: That's a good plan. If I **get back** anything, I'm thinking of using it to **catch up** on some overdue bills first. But I might also **splurge** a little on a weekend getaway.

Jack: Hey, you deserve it! It's nice to **treat yourself** once in a while. But yeah, paying off debt is always the priority. I'm just hoping I **get my refund** before summer so I can plan a trip.

Emily: Same here! The sooner the better. I'll be sure to **track** my refund status online just to make sure everything goes smoothly.

Glossary

File: To submit documents, especially tax returns, to the proper authorities.

Submit: To officially send something, such as forms or documents.

Get back: To receive something after sending or waiting for it (e.g., money, refund).

Help out: To assist or provide support, often with money.

Look forward to: To anticipate or eagerly await something.

Get a good amount: To receive a substantial or favorable sum of money.

Get by: To manage or survive, often with limited resources.

Add up: To accumulate or total a certain amount.

Break even: To neither lose nor gain money; to reach a point of balance.

Spend: To use money for goods or services.

Pay off: To fully settle or clear a debt or loan.

Knock out: To complete or finish something, often with effort.

Catch up: To get back to a normal or balanced state, often after falling behind.

Splurge: To spend money on something extravagant or non-essential.
Treat yourself: To reward oneself, often with something enjoyable.
Track: To follow the progress or status of something, like a shipment or refund.

Speaking time
What do you usually do with your tax refund? Do you use it to pay off debts, save, or spend it on something fun?
How important is it for you to keep receipts and track your expenses during the year for tax purposes? Why?

Budgeting for a Family

Jake: Hey, Amy! I've been meaning to ask—how do you and Mike **stay on top of** your family budget? It feels like we're always **running out of** money before the month's over.

Amy: Oh, trust me, it took us a while to **get the hang of** it. We sat down and **laid out** all our expenses. Once we figured out where our money was going, we could **cut back on** unnecessary stuff.

Jake: That makes sense. We definitely need to **cut down on** eating out. It's so easy to grab takeout when we're busy, but it really **adds up**.

Amy: Exactly! We started **cooking at home** more, and it's saved us a ton. Plus, we made a plan to **set aside** a bit of money each month for emergencies.

Jake: That's a smart move. We've been trying to **pay off** some credit card debt, so saving feels impossible.

Amy: You just have to **start small**. Even $50 a month can make a difference. And don't forget to **shop around** for deals. We've been **keeping an eye out for** sales and using apps to track discounts.

Jake: I hadn't thought about that. I'm usually in such a rush that I just **pick up** whatever we need without checking prices.

Amy: Oh, I've been there. But now, we **stick to** a shopping list and avoid impulse buys. It's all about **staying on track** with your priorities.

Jake: I guess it's about being disciplined, huh? Maybe I'll sit down with Sarah this weekend and **go over** everything.

Amy: Definitely! And don't beat yourself up if you have slip-ups. It's all part of the process. Once you've got a system, you'll feel so much better about your finances.

Glossary:
Stay on top of: To remain in control or well-informed about something.
Running out of: To have no more of something.
Get the hang of: To learn or understand how to do something.
Laid out: To plan or organize something in detail.
Cut back on: To reduce the amount of something.
Cut down on: To reduce the quantity or frequency of something.
Adds up: To accumulate or increase over time.
Set aside: To save or reserve something for a specific purpose.
Pay off: To finish paying a debt.
Shop around: To compare prices before making a purchase.
Keeping an eye out for: To watch for something specific.
Pick up: To buy or collect something.
Stick to: To follow or adhere to something.
Staying on track: To remain focused on a goal or plan.

Go over: To review or examine something in detail.

Speaking time

How do you usually budget for your expenses, and what changes could you make to save more money?

Do you think it's easier to stick to a budget when you have a family or when you're single? Why?

Living Paycheck to Paycheck

Lisa: Hey, Rob, you look stressed. Everything okay?

Rob: Honestly, Lisa, I'm just overwhelmed. I've been **living paycheck to paycheck**, and it feels like I'm barely **keeping my head above water**.

Lisa: Oh, I hear you. I've been there before. Every time I'd **put away** a little money, something would come up and wipe it out.

Rob: Exactly! Last month, I had to **shell out** for car repairs, and now my credit card bill is through the roof. It's like I can't **catch a break**.

Lisa: I know it's tough, but have you tried **breaking down** your expenses? When I did that, I realized I was spending a lot on things I didn't really need, like streaming services I didn't even watch.

Rob: Yeah, I've thought about it, but it's hard to find the time to sit down and **go over** everything.

Lisa: Trust me, it's worth it. Once you **figure out** where your money is going, you can **cut back on** the extras. I even started meal prepping to **cut down on** takeout.

Rob: That's smart. I've been trying to **pick up extra hours** at work, but it's exhausting.

Lisa: I get that, but don't burn yourself out. Maybe look into side gigs or ways to **bring in** some passive income.

Rob: Yeah, I've thought about freelancing, but it feels overwhelming.

Lisa: Start small! And don't forget to **reach out to** your credit card company. Sometimes they'll **work out** a lower interest rate if you ask.
Rob: I hadn't thought of that. I'll give them a call. I just hate feeling like I'm **stuck in a rut**.
Lisa: You're not stuck—you're just in a tough spot. It's all about making small changes and sticking to them. You'll **turn things around** eventually.

Glossary:
Living paycheck to paycheck: Using most or all of your income to cover expenses, with little or no savings.
Keeping my head above water: Managing to survive despite financial difficulties.
Put away: To save or store something, like money.
Shell out: To spend money, often reluctantly.
Catch a break: To experience good luck or a reprieve from challenges.
Breaking down: Analyzing or separating something into smaller parts.
Go over: To review or examine in detail.
Figure out: To understand or determine something.
Cut back on: To reduce or limit something.
Cut down on: To decrease the amount or frequency of something.
Pick up extra hours: To work more hours than usual.
Bring in: To earn or generate money.

Reach out to: To contact or ask for help from someone.
Work out: To negotiate or resolve something.
Stuck in a rut: Feeling trapped in a boring or unproductive situation.
Turn things around: To improve a situation.

Speaking time
What would you do to reduce your expenses if you were living paycheck to paycheck?
Do you think budgeting or finding extra income is more effective for financial stability? Why?

Investing in Stocks and Bonds

Jack: Hey, Emily, I've been thinking about **getting into** investing. Do you know much about stocks and bonds?

Emily: Oh yeah, I started investing a couple of years ago. At first, I was scared to **jump in**, but now I'm glad I did.

Jack: That's where I'm at. I don't want to **mess up** and lose money, though.

Emily: Totally get that. I did a lot of research before I **put in** my first dollar. I started small, just to **test the waters**.

Jack: What kind of stuff did you invest in?

Emily: A mix. I've got some stocks that I think will **pay off** in the long run and a few bonds that are steady but not as exciting.

Jack: Stocks sound risky. Did you ever **lose out on** anything?

Emily: Oh, for sure! There were times when the market went down, and I thought I'd **blown it**, but I just had to **ride it out**. The key is not to **freak out** when things dip.

Jack: That sounds easier said than done. What about bonds?

Emily: They're more predictable, but the returns aren't as high. It's good to **spread out** your investments so you're not putting all your eggs in one basket.

Jack: That makes sense. Did you use an app or a financial advisor to **figure out** what to invest in?

Emily: I started with an app, but later I **reached out to** a financial advisor for some advice. They helped me **sort through** my options and come up with a plan.

Jack: Sounds like a solid approach. I'll definitely need to **brush up on** my knowledge before I dive in.

Emily: Definitely. And don't forget to **keep an eye on** your portfolio, but don't obsess over it. Sometimes, you just have to let your investments **work for you**.

Jack: Good advice. Thanks, Emily. I think I'll start small and see how it goes.

Emily: That's the way to go. You'll **get the hang of it** in no time.

Glossary:
Getting into: Becoming involved in something.
Jump in: To start something quickly or enthusiastically.
Mess up: To make a mistake or do something poorly.
Put in: To invest or allocate money.
Test the waters: To try something out to see if it works.
Pay off: To result in success or benefit.
Lose out on: To miss an opportunity or suffer a loss.
Blown it: Made a big mistake.
Ride it out: To endure or wait through a difficult time.
Freak out: To panic or get very upset.
Spread out: To diversify or distribute.

Figure out: To understand or solve something.
Reach out to: To contact someone for help or advice.
Sort through: To organize or decide among options.
Brush up on: To refresh your knowledge or skills.
Keep an eye on: To monitor or watch something closely.
Work for you: To function effectively without much effort.
Get the hang of it: To learn or understand how to do something.

Speaking time

What would you invest in if you had extra money, and why?
Do you think stocks or bonds are a better option for long-term investing? Why?

Saving for Retirement

Mark: Hey, Lisa, have you started thinking about retirement?

Lisa: Oh, absolutely! I've been trying to **set aside** some money every month, but it's tough with all the bills.

Mark: I hear you. It feels like there's always something that **comes up**, right? But I've been trying to **stick to** a budget so I can save more.

Lisa: That's smart. Do you have a specific plan?

Mark: Kind of. I've been putting money into a 401(k), and I'm also trying to **build up** an emergency fund. I don't want to **dip into** my retirement savings for unexpected expenses.

Lisa: That's a good call. I'm still trying to **figure out** how much I need to retire comfortably. It's hard to plan so far ahead.

Mark: Totally. I've been using one of those online calculators to **map out** my goals. It's not perfect, but it gives me an idea of how much I should be saving.

Lisa: That's a great idea. I've been thinking about meeting with a financial advisor to **lay out** a solid plan.

Mark: You should! Mine helped me **sort through** all my options, like IRAs and different investments. It really **paid off** because now I feel more confident about my future.

Lisa: I guess I just need to **get started**. I've been putting it off because it feels overwhelming.

Mark: That's normal, but the sooner you **jump into** it, the better. Even small contributions can **add up** over time.

Lisa: True. I think I'll start by cutting back on some unnecessary spending and **putting away** the extra cash.

Mark: That's the way to do it. Just take it one step at a time, and you'll **get the hang of it**.

Glossary:
Set aside: To save or reserve money or resources.
Comes up: To arise or occur unexpectedly.
Stick to: To follow or adhere to a plan or decision.
Build up: To increase or accumulate.
Dip into: To use a portion of saved resources.
Figure out: To understand or determine something.
Map out: To plan or organize in detail.
Lay out: To explain or arrange systematically.
Sort through: To examine and organize options or items.
Paid off: To result in success or benefit.
Get started: To begin something.
Put off: To delay or procrastinate.
Jump into: To start something quickly or without hesitation.
Add up: To accumulate or grow gradually.
Putting away: Saving or storing something for future use.

Get the hang of it: To learn or become familiar with something.

Speaking time

Do you think it's better to start saving for retirement early, or focus on other priorities first? Why?

What steps would you take to prepare for retirement if you were starting from scratch?

Buying vs. Renting a Home

Jessica: So, Michael, have you thought about **settling down** and buying a house yet?

Michael: I have, but I'm still on the fence. Renting has been working out for me, and I don't want to **jump into** something I'm not ready for.

Jessica: That makes sense, but I've been trying to **save up** for a down payment. It feels like throwing money away when I pay rent every month.

Michael: True, but with renting, I don't have to worry about repairs or unexpected costs. Last year, my fridge broke, and the landlord had to **take care of** it.

Jessica: That's a perk, for sure. But owning a home is an investment. You can build equity and eventually **pay it off** instead of paying someone else.

Michael: I get that, but I'm not sure I'm ready to **take on** a mortgage. It's such a big commitment, and I'd hate to **get stuck** in one place.

Jessica: That's fair. Buying is definitely a long-term move. Have you thought about **checking out** first-time homebuyer programs? They can help with the upfront costs.

Michael: I've looked into it, but I still think renting gives me more flexibility. Plus, I don't have to **shell out** for property taxes or maintenance.

Jessica: That's a good point. I guess it depends on your lifestyle. I'm looking for stability, so I'm ready to **settle down**.

Michael: Maybe I'll rethink it in a few years. For now, I'll **stick with** renting and keep saving for when I'm ready to make the leap.

Glossary:
Settling down: Establishing a permanent place or lifestyle.
On the fence: Undecided or unsure about something.
Jump into: To start something quickly or without careful consideration.
Save up: To accumulate money for a specific purpose.
Take care of: To handle or resolve something.
Pay it off: To completely repay a loan or debt.
Take on: To accept or assume responsibility for something.
Get stuck: To be unable to leave or escape a situation.
Checking out: To look into or investigate something.
Shell out: To pay money, often reluctantly.
Settle down: To establish a stable life, often in a permanent home.
Stick with: To continue with or choose to stay with something.

Speaking time

What do you think are the biggest advantages of buying a home compared to renting?

If you were choosing between buying or renting, what factors would influence your decision the most?

Starting a Side Hustle

Emily: Hey, Jake! I've been meaning to ask—didn't you say you wanted to **start up** a side hustle?

Jake: Yeah, I've been thinking about it. I just need to figure out what I can **pull off** with my schedule.

Emily: That's key. You don't want to **bite off more than you can chew**. What kind of ideas are you tossing around?

Jake: Well, I've been thinking about **picking up** freelance graphic design. I already have the skills, so why not **cash in on** them?

Emily: That's a great idea! You could also **reach out to** small businesses. They're always looking for affordable design work.

Jake: True. I just need to **set up** a portfolio and maybe a website to show off my work.

Emily: Totally! And don't forget to **spread the word**. Let your friends and family know you're taking on projects—they might know someone who needs help.

Jake: Good point. I'm also worried about finding the time. I don't want it to **eat into** my full-time job or weekends.

Emily: That's the tricky part, but if you **map out** your schedule, you can make it work. Just don't burn yourself out.
Jake: Right, I've heard that can happen fast. I think I'll **test the waters** with one or two projects before diving in completely.
Emily: Smart move! Once you **get the hang of it**, you'll know if it's worth expanding.
Jake: Thanks for the advice, Emily. I think I'm ready to **take the plunge** and give it a shot!
Emily: Go for it! You've got what it takes.

Glossary:
Start up: To begin or launch something, like a business.
Pull off: To manage or accomplish something, often challenging.
Bite off more than you can chew: To take on more responsibilities than you can handle.
Picking up: To begin or take on something new.
Cash in on: To take advantage of an opportunity to make money.
Reach out to: To contact or approach someone.
Set up: To create or establish something.
Spread the word: To let people know about something.
Eat into: To use up time, money, or resources.
Map out: To plan something carefully.
Burn yourself out: To exhaust yourself by overworking.
Test the waters: To try something on a small scale before committing fully.

Get the hang of it: To become skilled or comfortable with something.
Take the plunge: To decide to do something significant, often after hesitation.

Speaking time
If you were to start a side hustle, what kind of work would you choose and why?
How would you balance a side hustle with your current responsibilities?

Paying Off Student Loans

Rachel: Hey, Kevin! You look like you're deep in thought. What's on your mind?

Kevin: Oh, just trying to figure out how to **pay off** my student loans faster. They're really **weighing me down**.

Rachel: I hear you. Those things can feel like a ball and chain. Have you thought about **chipping away at** the balance little by little?

Kevin: Yeah, I've been trying to **cut back on** my spending so I can throw more money at them each month.

Rachel: That's smart. Maybe you can **pick up** a side gig for extra cash. My cousin started delivering food on weekends, and it really **paid off** for her.

Kevin: I thought about that, but I don't want to **burn out**. My full-time job is already pretty demanding.

Rachel: That's fair. Another idea is to **look into** refinancing. It could lower your interest rate and make the payments more manageable.

Kevin: I actually **checked that out** last month, but my credit score isn't quite where it needs to be yet.
Rachel: Gotcha. Well, every little bit helps. Even putting an extra $50 toward your loans can make a big difference over time.
Kevin: True. I've also been thinking about setting up automatic payments. I've heard some lenders will **knock off** a bit of interest if you do that.
Rachel: Definitely! Plus, it's one less thing to worry about each month.
Kevin: Thanks for the tips, Rachel. I guess I just have to **stick with it** and stay patient.
Rachel: You've got this, Kevin. Just keep your eye on the prize—being debt-free feels amazing.

Glossary:
Pay off: To fully repay a debt.
Weighing me down: Making someone feel burdened or stressed.
Chipping away at: Gradually reducing or dealing with something.
Cut back on: To reduce spending or use of something.
Pick up: To start or take on a new job or task.
Paid off: To have a positive result, especially financially.
Burn out: To become overly tired or stressed from work or effort.
Look into: To research or investigate something.
Checked that out: Investigated or explored an option.

Knock off: To reduce or subtract, especially money.
Stick with it: To persist or continue working on something.

Speaking time
What strategies would you use to pay off a large debt like student loans?
Do you think taking on a side gig is worth it to pay off debt faster? Why or why not?

Teaching Kids About Money

Emily: Hey, Matt! I saw you at the store with your kids the other day. They looked excited about those toys in their hands.
Matt: Oh, yeah. We were practicing how to **budget**. I gave them each ten bucks and told them they had to **stick to it**.
Emily: That's awesome! Teaching them about money early on really **pays off** in the long run. Did they **catch on**?
Matt: Surprisingly, yes. My son even **put back** one of the toys when he realized he couldn't **cover** the cost. I was impressed.
Emily: That's great! I've been trying to teach my daughter about saving, but she always wants to **blow her money** as soon as she gets it.
Matt: Same here at first. I started giving them jars labeled "spend," "save," and "give." Now, they **set aside** some money for the future and even for charity.

Emily: That's such a good idea. My parents used to just **shell out** cash whenever I asked, so I didn't really learn how to manage it until later.

Matt: Same! That's why I want my kids to **figure out** the value of money early. We also play games where they have to **come up with** a plan to earn extra allowance.

Emily: Oh, that's clever. What kind of chores do they do?

Matt: Stuff like mowing the lawn, washing the car, and even helping out with groceries. They're really starting to **pick up on** how hard you have to work for money.

Emily: That's fantastic. I think I'll try some of those tips with my daughter. Maybe we'll **kick off** with the jar idea this weekend.

Matt: You should! It's amazing to see them learn. It's like watching little lightbulbs go off.

Emily: Thanks for the advice, Matt. I'll **give it a shot** and let you know how it goes!

Matt: Anytime!

Glossary:
Budget: To plan how to spend money.
Stick to it: To follow a plan or rule without deviating.
Pays off: To have a positive result or reward.
Catch on: To understand or grasp an idea.
Put back: To return something to its original place.
Cover: To have enough money to pay for something.

Blow her money: To spend money quickly and recklessly.
Set aside: To save or reserve something, such as money.
Shell out: To spend or give money, often reluctantly.
Figure out: To understand or solve something.
Come up with: To think of or create an idea or plan.
Pick up on: To notice or understand something.
Kick off: To start something.
Give it a shot: To try something new.

Speaking time

What do you think is the most important money lesson to teach kids?

How would you introduce the concept of saving to a child?

Living on a Tight Budget

Sarah: Hey, Jake! How's it going? You look a little stressed.
Jake: Oh, you know, just trying to **make ends meet**. Living on a tight budget isn't exactly a walk in the park.
Sarah: I hear you. I had to **cut back on** so many things last year when I was between jobs. It's tough, but you'll **get through it**.
Jake: Yeah, I've already started to **cut down on** eating out and unnecessary subscriptions. But something always seems to **come up**—car repairs, medical bills—you name it.

Sarah: Tell me about it. Last month, I had to **dip into** my emergency fund when my fridge broke down. It's like you take one step forward and two steps back.

Jake: Exactly! I've been trying to **figure out** ways to save more, but it's hard when every penny is already accounted for.

Sarah: Have you thought about **picking up** a side gig? Even a few extra bucks a week can help.

Jake: I have, actually. A friend of mine suggested I try delivering food on weekends. It's not ideal, but it could help me **stay afloat**.

Sarah: That's a good idea! And maybe you can **sell off** some things you don't use anymore. I made a couple hundred bucks selling old furniture online.

Jake: That's not a bad idea. I have a ton of stuff lying around that I could probably **get rid of**.

Sarah: See? There you go. And don't forget to look for coupons or deals when you shop. I **stock up on** non-perishables whenever they're on sale.

Jake: Thanks, Sarah. I really appreciate the tips. It's hard to stay positive, but I know I'll **pull through**.

Sarah: You've got this, Jake. Just take it one step at a time.

Jake: Thanks. I'll definitely try out some of these ideas.

Glossary:

Make ends meet: To manage financially with the money you have.
Cut back on: To reduce spending or usage.
Get through it: To overcome a challenge or tough situation.
Cut down on: To use or do less of something.
Come up: To arise or happen unexpectedly.
Dip into: To use savings or money set aside for emergencies.
Figure out: To solve or understand something.
Picking up: To take on a new task or job.
Stay afloat: To manage to survive financially.
Sell off: To sell items, often to raise money.
Get rid of: To remove or dispose of something.
Stock up on: To buy a large quantity of something.
Pull through: To survive or overcome a difficult time.

Speaking time

What strategies do you think are most effective for saving money when living on a tight budget?

Have you ever had to make a significant sacrifice to manage your finances? What was it?

Using Credit Wisely

Alex: Hey, Sam, have you ever had trouble **keeping up with** your credit card payments?

Sam: Oh, definitely. I used to **rack up** a lot of debt without even realizing it. It was hard to **get ahead** until I started paying closer attention.

Alex: Yeah, I know what you mean. I used to **charge up** everything, but then I realized I was only **digging myself into** a deeper hole. I had to **scale back on** my spending.

Sam: That's smart. I've learned to **stick to** a budget, but it's still tempting sometimes. I try to **hold off on** big purchases unless I really need them.

Alex: That's a good strategy. I also try to **pay off** my balance in full every month so I don't **rack up** interest. It makes a big difference in the long run.

Sam: I've been doing that too. It's hard at first, but once you get used to it, it's easier to **keep track of** your finances. I also **keep an eye on** my credit score so I don't **fall behind**.

Alex: Exactly. Keeping your credit score up is key, especially if you ever need to **take out** a loan. And remember, it's important to **shop around** for the best interest rates if you're planning to **borrow** money.

Sam: Totally. I've learned the hard way that some credit cards **charge you up** with high interest rates. So now, I only use cards that offer rewards or lower rates.

Alex: Smart move! The key is really to **manage** your credit well. That way, you can **avoid getting stuck** with high debt.

Sam: Absolutely. I'm definitely more careful now. I just need to **stay on top of** things and keep working on **paying down** what I owe.

Glossary:
Keeping up with: To manage or stay current with something.
Rack up: To accumulate (often used for debt or expenses).
Get ahead: To make progress or improve your financial situation.
Charge up: To put expenses on a credit card.
Dig yourself into: To get deeper into a negative situation.
Scale back on: To reduce the amount of something, usually spending.
Stick to: To follow or stay committed to something.
Hold off on: To delay or postpone a decision or action.
Pay off: To repay in full (usually a debt or loan).
Rack up: To accumulate, especially in terms of money or debt.
Keep track of: To monitor or record something.
Keep an eye on: To watch or monitor something closely.
Fall behind: To fail to keep up with something, like payments or deadlines.
Take out: To borrow money, typically through a loan or credit.
Shop around: To compare prices, deals, or options.

Borrow: To take and use something with the intention of returning it.
Charge you up: To apply high interest rates.
Manage: To control or handle something, like finances.
Avoid getting stuck: To prevent finding yourself in a difficult situation.
Stay on top of: To manage and stay in control of something.
Paying down: To reduce the amount of debt or loan.

Speaking time
What are some strategies you use to manage your credit wisely?
Have you ever found it difficult to avoid using credit, and how did you handle it?

The Cost of Higher Education

Chris: Hey, Rachel, have you been looking into the **costs of** college lately? It's crazy how much tuition has **gone up**.

Rachel: Oh, tell me about it! I've been trying to **figure out** how I'm going to **come up with** the money. Between tuition, books, and living expenses, it's all adding up fast.

Chris: I know! I've been **looking into** financial aid options, but it's not easy to **get approved for** grants or scholarships. It feels like they're getting harder to come by.

Rachel: Yeah, I tried to **apply for** a few scholarships last year, but I didn't get anything. Now I'm considering taking out a loan, but I'm really worried about how long it will **take to pay off**.

Chris: That's the thing. The debt can **stack up** over time, especially if you don't **get through** your degree quickly. I've heard people say they're still paying off their student loans even ten years after graduation!

Rachel: That's so scary. I really want to **avoid** that, but sometimes it feels like there's no other choice. Have you thought about **going for** a part-time job? Maybe that would help with the expenses.

Chris: I've thought about it, but I'm already **juggling** a full course load, so I'm not sure I can **fit in** a job too. I'm trying to **cut back on** unnecessary expenses, like eating out or buying new clothes.

Rachel: Yeah, that's smart. I've been **looking at** cheaper housing options too. I want to **cut down on** rent as much as possible. Maybe I'll even have to **move in with** some roommates to make ends meet.

Chris: That's probably the way to go. The cost of living is ridiculous these days. I've been **trying to figure out** how to **balance** work and school, but it's tough.

Rachel: Totally. I think we just need to **keep an eye on** opportunities and **stay on top of** our budgets. Otherwise, it's easy to **fall behind** on payments.

Chris: Agreed. The key is to **stay organized** and plan ahead. We'll figure it out!

Glossary:
Costs of: The total amount of money needed for something.
Gone up: Increased or become more expensive.
Figure out: To solve or understand something.
Come up with: To think of or produce an idea or solution.
Looking into: Investigating or researching something.
Get approved for: To be accepted or accepted for something, such as a loan or grant.
Apply for: To formally request or seek something.
Take out: To borrow, usually money (as in loans).

Take to pay off: The time required to fully repay a loan or debt.
Stack up: To accumulate or increase.
Get through: To finish or complete something, often an education or project.
Avoid: To prevent or keep away from.
Going for: Trying to obtain or aim for something.
Juggling: Managing multiple things or tasks at once.
Fit in: To make time for something within an existing schedule.
Cut back on: To reduce the amount of something, especially spending.
Looking at: Considering or thinking about something.
Cut down on: To reduce or limit something.
Move in with: To live in the same place as someone, typically roommates or family.
Make ends meet: To manage financially, often with difficulty.
Stay on top of: To manage something effectively, especially keeping up with tasks.
Fall behind: To not keep up with something, such as payments or deadlines.
Stay organized: To keep things orderly and manage tasks well.

Speaking time
What are some ways you manage to save money when it comes to education costs?
Do you think student loans are worth it in the long run? Why or why not?

The Impact of Inflation

Jake: Hey Sarah, have you noticed how much prices have **gone up** lately? I mean, groceries are getting more expensive by the day.
Sarah: Oh, I know! It's crazy. I had to **cut back on** some of my usual purchases because of inflation. Even basic things like bread and milk are more expensive.
Jake: I hear you. I've been **keeping an eye on** my spending. Every time I go to the store, I feel like I'm **spending more than I expected**. It's like I can't **keep up with** rising costs.
Sarah: It's definitely tough. And the worst part is that wages aren't really **keeping pace with** inflation. It feels like I'm working harder but my paycheck isn't stretching as far.
Jake: Exactly! I've also had to **rethink** how I manage my finances. I'm trying to **put aside** a little extra money every month to deal with higher prices, but it's not easy.
Sarah: Same here. I've been **looking for** cheaper alternatives for things I usually buy. It's all about trying to **make do with** less.
Jake: Have you noticed how much the cost of gas has **shot up**? It's making it harder to **get by** from week to week. I'm considering cutting back on trips to save some money.

Sarah: I've had to **skip out on** some of my regular outings because of gas prices. It's a real pain, but what else can we do? We've just got to **weather the storm** until things get better.
Jake: I guess so. I'm trying to **stay optimistic** and hope that inflation will **slow down** soon. But in the meantime, we'll have to **tighten our belts** a bit more.
Sarah: Yeah, it's all about adjusting to the times. We just need to **hang in there** and take it one day at a time.

Glossary:
Gone up: Increased or become more expensive.
Cut back on: To reduce the amount of something.
Keeping an eye on: Monitoring or watching something carefully.
Spending more than expected: Paying more than planned or anticipated.
Keep up with: To continue matching or managing, especially with increasing costs.
Rethink: To reconsider or change one's approach or decisions.
Put aside: To save or reserve something, especially money.
Looking for: Searching or trying to find something, like alternatives.
Make do with: To manage with what you have, even if it's not ideal.
Shot up: Increased rapidly or suddenly.
Get by: To manage to live or function, especially with limited resources.

Skip out on: To miss or avoid something, often intentionally.
Weather the storm: To endure a difficult or challenging situation.
Stay optimistic: To remain positive or hopeful about the future.
Slow down: To decrease in speed or intensity, like inflation.
Tighten our belts: To reduce expenses or live more frugally.
Hang in there: To persevere or continue despite difficulties.

Speaking time
How does inflation affect your daily life, and what do you do to cope with it?
Do you think the government should do more to address inflation? Why or why not?

Financing a Vacation

Emily: Hey, Matt, have you started planning your vacation yet? I was thinking about taking a trip this summer, but I'm not sure how I'm going to **come up with** the money for it.

Matt: Oh, I hear you. I've been **putting off** booking my trip too. It's tough to **save up for** a vacation these days.

Emily: Exactly. I've been **cutting back on** some things, like eating out, to try and **save up** a little more. But even then, I'm still not sure if I can **pull it off**.

Matt: I've been thinking about **looking into** some options, like taking out a small loan or maybe **charging** the trip to my credit card. I know it's not ideal, but sometimes you just have to **go for it**.

Emily: Hmm, I don't know. I'm a little hesitant to **charge** the entire vacation, but I've been thinking about **splitting** the costs between my credit card and my savings. That way, I can **take care of** some of it now and the rest later.

Matt: Yeah, that sounds like a good plan. I've also been **trying to figure out** how to get a deal on flights and hotels to **cut down on** expenses. Have you tried looking for any discounts?

Emily: Oh, for sure. I've been **keeping an eye on** travel deals for a while now. I've also been **searching for** promo codes and trying to **take advantage of** any sales.

Matt: That's smart. I've been **setting aside** a little extra money each month, too, just in case I need a bit more to **cover** everything. It's tough, but it'll be worth it once I'm lying on the beach!

Emily: Totally! I'm hoping to **cash in on** some points from my credit card too. If I can get a few perks, it'll make the trip a lot more affordable.

Matt: Sounds like you've got it all figured out. Maybe I should **follow your lead** and start saving a little more aggressively.

Emily: Well, we'll both have to **keep our fingers crossed** that we can pull this off without going broke!

Glossary:
Come up with: To find or think of an idea or money.
Putting off: Delaying or postponing something.
Save up: To accumulate money over time.
Pull it off: To successfully accomplish something, especially when it's difficult.

Looking into: Investigating or considering an option.
Charging: Using a credit card to pay for something.
Go for it: To take the opportunity or risk, often with enthusiasm.
Splitting: Dividing the cost between different sources.
Take care of: To handle or deal with something.
Trying to figure out: Trying to solve or make sense of something.
Cut down on: To reduce the amount of something.
Keeping an eye on: Watching or monitoring something closely.
Searching for: Looking for something, usually something specific.
Take advantage of: To use something for your benefit.
Setting aside: Saving or reserving something for later.
Cover: To pay for or take responsibility for something.
Cash in on: To benefit or profit from something, often by using points or rewards.
Follow your lead: To imitate or do what someone else is doing.
Keep our fingers crossed: Hoping for a positive outcome.

Speaking time

How do you typically finance your vacations, and what strategies do you use to save for them?

Would you prefer to pay for a vacation upfront or charge it to a credit card and pay later? Why?

Dealing with Unexpected Expenses

Sarah: Hey, Mark, you won't believe what happened. I just had to **shell out** a ton of money for my car repairs. Totally unexpected!

Mark: Ugh, that's the worst. I've had a few of those moments lately. Sometimes it feels like you're just **waiting for** the next surprise expense to pop up.

Sarah: I know, right? I was doing fine with my budget, but then this huge bill came out of nowhere. I had to **dig into** my savings to **cover** it.

Mark: Man, that's tough. I had to **pick up** some extra shifts last month to make up for a surprise medical bill. It's hard to **keep up with** all these extra costs.

Sarah: I hear you. I've been **cutting back on** some things to make sure I can **stay on top of** my other bills. But it's frustrating—sometimes it feels like I'll never get ahead.

Mark: Yeah, it's like you're always **playing catch-up**. But have you thought about **setting aside** a little extra each month for emergencies? That way, it's easier to **bounce back** when something unexpected happens.

Sarah: I've been trying to, but it's hard to **stick to** it. Sometimes, even when I try to **save up**, something always comes up.

Mark: I get it. It's tough to **plan for** the unexpected. But maybe you could try **building up** an emergency fund that you only use for these kinds of things. It might help **ease the stress** a bit.

Sarah: That's a good idea. I've heard a lot about people who **set aside** a certain amount each paycheck just for emergencies. I should really **stick with** that plan.

Mark: For sure. It's not always easy, but it definitely makes life a little easier when the unexpected happens.

Glossary:
Shell out: To spend a large amount of money, often unexpectedly.
Waiting for: Anticipating or expecting something to happen.

Dig into: To use part of your savings or resources for something.
Cover: To pay for something, typically an unexpected expense.
Pick up: To do extra work, often to make up for an unexpected expense.
Keep up with: To manage or stay on top of responsibilities or payments.
Cutting back on: Reducing spending or consumption.
Stay on top of: To manage or keep control of tasks or finances.
Playing catch-up: Trying to deal with tasks or responsibilities that have been delayed or neglected.
Setting aside: Saving or reserving money for a specific purpose.
Bounce back: To recover from a setback or difficulty.
Stick to: To continue doing something consistently.
Plan for: To prepare for something that may happen in the future.
Building up: Accumulating or saving money or resources over time.
Ease the stress: To reduce pressure or worry.

Speaking time
How do you usually prepare for unexpected expenses? Do you have an emergency fund?
Have you ever had to deal with a major unexpected expense? How did you handle it?

Choosing the Right Insurance

Emma: Hey, Jason, I've been thinking about getting insurance for my car, but I'm not sure where to **start off**. There are so many options out there.

Jason: Yeah, it can be overwhelming. I had the same issue last year. I ended up **shopping around** for the best deal. Have you looked into what kind of coverage you need?

Emma: A little bit. I know I need something basic, but I'm not sure if I should **go for** a higher level of coverage. I don't want to **get stuck with** a huge bill if something happens, you know?

Jason: I totally get that. When I was in the same situation, I decided to **opt for** a policy with a higher deductible so I could **save up** on the premium. But if you have a high deductible, make sure you can **cover** it if something unexpected happens.
Emma: That's a good point. I guess I should **look into** the details more closely. I don't want to **end up** paying for coverage I don't need.
Jason: Exactly. A lot of times, people just **go with** the first option that sounds good, but you need to **weigh up** the pros and cons before deciding. I also had to **figure out** how much coverage I really needed for my car and whether I should **add on** things like roadside assistance.
Emma: Oh, I didn't even think about that! It's good to **think ahead**. I don't want to **regret** my choice later.
Jason: For sure. It's all about finding a balance between what you need and what you can afford. And don't forget to **check out** customer reviews. Sometimes, insurance companies seem great until you actually **file** a claim.
Emma: I'll definitely **look into** that before I make any decisions. Thanks for the advice, Jason.
Jason: No problem! Glad I could help. Good luck with choosing the right one!

Glossary:
Start off: To begin or initiate something.

Shopping around: Comparing different options to find the best deal.
Go for: To choose or select something.
Get stuck with: To end up with something undesirable or difficult to deal with.
Opt for: To choose a particular option.
Save up: To set aside money for a future purpose.
Cover: To be financially responsible for something, especially expenses.
Look into: To investigate or research something.
End up: To eventually arrive at a final result or situation.
Go with: To choose something or make a decision.
Weigh up: To carefully consider and evaluate different options.
Figure out: To solve or understand something.
Add on: To include something extra.
Think ahead: To plan for the future.
Regret: To feel bad or sorry about a decision or action.
Check out: To examine or review something.
File: To officially submit a document, especially for insurance claims.

Speaking time

What factors do you consider when choosing insurance?
Have you ever had to deal with an insurance claim? How did it go?

Planning a Wedding on a Budget

Samantha: Hey, Emily, have you started **figuring out** the details for your wedding yet? I know you've been engaged for a little while now.

Emily: I've been **thinking about** it a lot, but I really want to **keep it simple**. Weddings can get so expensive, and I don't want to **blow all our savings** on one day.

Samantha: I totally understand. When I was planning mine, I had to **cut back** on a lot of things. We decided to **skip** a big venue and just have a small ceremony at a local park. It worked out great and saved us a ton of money.
Emily: That's a great idea. I was also **looking into** cheaper venues, but I'm not sure where to **start off**. Do you think it's better to **go for** a DIY wedding or hire vendors for everything?
Samantha: Honestly, if you're **working with** a budget, I'd say **go for** the DIY option for things like decorations and invitations. But for the big stuff, like the catering and photographer, it's probably better to **splurge a little**.
Emily: Yeah, I was thinking the same thing. I definitely don't want to **skimp on** the food or photos. How did you **manage to** get the best deals for vendors?
Samantha: I just **asked around** and **looked up** reviews online. There are a lot of affordable options, but you have to **be willing to** compromise a little. I also asked family and friends if they could help out, and some offered to **pitch in** for certain things.
Emily: That's such a smart idea. I think I might need to **ask for** help with the decorations. I'm not really **good at** DIY projects, but if my mom helps, we could **pull it off**.
Samantha: Exactly! And don't forget to **shop around** for deals. You can find great discounts on wedding dresses and even bouquets if you **keep an eye out**.

Emily: I'll definitely do that. Thanks for all the advice! I feel more confident about sticking to my budget now.

Samantha: No problem! You've got this. Just remember to **enjoy** the process – it's a special time, even if it's not perfect.

Glossary:
Figuring out: To work out or decide on something.
Thinking about: To consider or plan something.
Keep it simple: To make things less complicated or expensive.
Blow all our savings: To spend a large amount of money, often too much.
Cut back: To reduce spending or the amount of something.
Skip: To avoid or not include something.
Looking into: To investigate or research something.
Start off: To begin or initiate something.
Go for: To choose or select something.
Working with: To deal with or use a certain amount of resources or budget.
Splurge a little: To spend money on something more expensive than usual.
Skimp on: To spend less or reduce the quality of something.
Manage to: To succeed in doing something, especially with difficulty.
Ask around: To ask multiple people for advice or information.

Look up: To search for information, typically online.
Be willing to: To be open or ready to do something.
Pitch in: To contribute or help out, especially with money or effort.
Ask for: To request something from someone.
Good at: To be skilled or proficient in something.
Pull it off: To succeed in doing something difficult or challenging.
Shop around: To compare prices or options before buying.
Keep an eye out: To watch for or look for something.
Enjoy: To take pleasure in something.

Speaking time

What are some tips you have for sticking to a budget while planning an event?

Have you ever had to plan something important on a tight budget? How did you manage it?

The Benefits of Cashback and Rewards Credit Cards

Jack: Hey, Sarah! I've been thinking about **signing up for** a rewards credit card. Have you used one before?

Sarah: Oh, definitely! I've had one for a while now. The cashback rewards are awesome, especially if you **keep track of** your spending. It's like getting a little bonus at the end of the month.

Jack: That sounds pretty great. I've heard that rewards cards can really **add up** if you use them regularly. But do they have any downsides?

Sarah: Well, the main thing is that you have to **stay on top of** your payments. If you **miss a payment**, the interest can really **cancel out** the rewards. But if you're responsible, they're totally worth it.

Jack: Yeah, I've heard about the interest thing. I definitely don't want to **fall behind** on my payments. What about the sign-up bonuses? Do those really **pay off**?

Sarah: Absolutely! Some cards offer huge sign-up bonuses if you **spend a certain amount** within the first few months. It's a great way to **get started** with rewards right away. I've actually **earned back** quite a bit just from the bonuses.

Jack: That's awesome. I've been looking at a few cards, and it looks like some of them **offer** cash back on certain categories like groceries or gas. Do you usually **stick with** the same category, or do you **mix it up**?

Sarah: I **mix it up**, depending on what's on sale or what I'm buying. Some cards even let you **switch categories** every quarter, so you can **take advantage of** different cashback offers. You just need to **plan ahead** a bit.

Jack: That's really helpful to know. I've always thought credit cards were more trouble than they were worth, but it sounds like if you're smart with them, they can actually **work out** in your favor.

Sarah: Exactly! Just make sure to **read the fine print** and **watch out for** any hidden fees. As long as you're careful, they can really **help out** in the long run.

Jack: Thanks for the tips! I'm definitely going to look into it more. I think I'll **sign up for** one of these cards soon.

Sarah: No problem, Jack! Let me know if you need any advice on which one to go for.

Glossary:
Signing up for: To register for or enroll in something, like a service or card.
Keep track of: To monitor or manage something over time.
Add up: To accumulate or increase in amount.
Stay on top of: To manage something well or keep up with it.
Miss a payment: To fail to pay on time.

Cancel out: To negate or undo the effect of something.
Fall behind: To not keep up with something, like payments.
Pay off: To result in a good outcome or reward.
Spend a certain amount: To use a specific amount of money within a given time.
Get started: To begin something, like using a rewards program.
Earn back: To recover or get back money spent, often through rewards.
Offer: To provide or give something, like cashback or rewards.
Stick with: To continue using or doing something.
Mix it up: To vary or change things instead of staying the same.
Switch categories: To change the types of purchases that earn rewards.
Take advantage of: To use something to your benefit.
Plan ahead: To prepare or organize something in advance.
Work out: To result in something favorable or successful.
Read the fine print: To carefully examine the details of a contract or agreement.
Watch out for: To be cautious of something, especially potential problems.
Help out: To assist or make something easier for someone.

Speaking time

How do you usually manage your credit card payments to avoid interest and fees?

Have you ever used a rewards or cashback credit card? What was your experience?

Understanding Cryptocurrency

Mike: Hey, Jessica! I've been hearing a lot about cryptocurrency lately. Do you know anything about it?

Jessica: Oh yeah, I've been **looking into** it for a while now. It's basically a digital form of money that isn't controlled by any government. It's pretty cool, but it can be confusing at first.

Mike: I'm with you on that. I'm still trying to **wrap my head around** how it works. What's the deal with Bitcoin?

Jessica: Bitcoin is the most popular cryptocurrency. It's a type of **digital currency** that you can **buy into** and hold, but it can also be used to make purchases online. The tricky part is that its value can **go up and down** really quickly.

Mike: That sounds a bit risky. Is it safe to **invest in**?

Jessica: Well, it's kind of a gamble, honestly. You have to **keep an eye on** the market because it can be volatile. But a lot of people have **made a killing** by getting in early. The key is to not **put all your eggs in one basket**.

Mike: Got it. So, if I **decide to** get into it, what do I need to know?

Jessica: First, you'll need a digital wallet to store your cryptocurrency. Then, you can **buy into** different coins or tokens on various platforms. But just be sure to **do your homework** before you invest, because it's easy to **fall for** scams in the crypto world.

Mike: Yikes, that's a bit scary. But I guess it's kind of like the stock market in that sense, right?

Jessica: Exactly! It's similar to stocks, but with much higher risk. You've got to **stay on top of** your investments and **watch out for** market changes. But if you're smart about it, it can **pay off** big time.

Mike: I'll definitely need to **learn more** before jumping in. Thanks for helping me **figure out** the basics!

Jessica: No problem! Just be sure to **take it slow** and **think twice** before you make any big moves. Crypto's fun, but it's not something to **dive into** without understanding it first.

Glossary:
Looking into: To investigate or study something.
Wrap my head around: To understand something that's complex or confusing.
Buy into: To purchase something, usually as an investment.
Go up and down: To fluctuate or change quickly in value or amount.
Invest in: To put money into something with the expectation of gaining a profit.

Keep an eye on: To monitor something carefully.
Made a killing: To make a large profit, usually quickly.
Put all your eggs in one basket: To risk everything on one plan or investment.
Decide to: To make a decision to do something.
Do your homework: To research or prepare for something thoroughly.
Fall for: To be tricked or deceived by something.
Stay on top of: To manage or keep up with something effectively.
Watch out for: To be cautious or aware of something.
Pay off: To result in a good outcome, often after hard work or risk.
Learn more: To gain further knowledge or information about something.
Figure out: To understand or solve something.
Take it slow: To approach something gradually and carefully.
Think twice: To reconsider or carefully consider something.
Dive into: To engage in something with full effort, often without much preparation.

Speaking time

What are some potential risks you should be aware of when investing in cryptocurrency?
How would you explain cryptocurrency to someone who has never heard of it?

Borrowing Money from Friends or Family

Sam: Hey, Chris. I need to **talk over** something with you. I'm in a bit of a financial bind, and I might need to **borrow** some money for a couple of weeks.

Chris: Oh no, Sam, I hope everything's okay. What happened?

Sam: Well, I had some unexpected bills come up, and now I'm trying to **catch up** on everything. I'm usually pretty good about managing my finances, but this one hit me out of nowhere.

Chris: I get it, man. It happens to the best of us. So, how much are you looking to **borrow**?

Sam: Just a couple hundred, enough to **cover** the bills until I get paid next week. I'll pay you back as soon as I can.

Chris: Okay, I understand. But just so you know, I'm not sure if I can **front** you the whole amount right now. I've got some things I need to **take care of** too.

Sam: Yeah, no worries. I totally get that. I was just hoping to **ask around** to see if I could **get a little help** until I'm back on track.

Chris: I get it. But borrowing money from family and friends can be tricky, man. You don't want things to **get awkward** later on if something goes wrong. Have you **thought about** a plan to pay it back?

Sam: Yeah, I've got it all **figured out**. I'll **pay you back** in full as soon as I get my paycheck. And if there's any problem, I'll let you know right away.

Chris: Alright, I'll help you out, but make sure to **stick to** your word. I don't want this to **come between** us if something goes wrong.

Sam: Of course, Chris. I really appreciate it, man. I'll **make sure** to **pay you back** on time.

Chris: No problem, just be careful next time. I don't want you to keep having to **rely on** others when things get tight.

Sam: I know, I've learned my lesson. I'll do my best to **stay ahead** next time.

Glossary:
Talk over: To discuss something with someone.
Borrow: To take something with the intention of returning it.
Catch up: To resolve a backlog or to return to a normal state.
Cover: To pay for something or to manage an expense.
Front: To provide or give money in advance.

Take care of: To handle or deal with something.
Ask around: To inquire or ask different people for help or information.
Get a little help: To seek assistance from someone.
Get awkward: To become uncomfortable, usually in a social situation.
Thought about: To consider or plan.
Figure out: To understand or solve something.
Stick to: To follow through with a plan or promise.
Come between: To cause tension or conflict in a relationship.
Make sure: To ensure something is done or happens.
Rely on: To depend on someone or something.
Stay ahead: To maintain control or be proactive about something.

Speaking time
How would you feel if a close friend asked to borrow money from you?
What do you think is the best way to handle borrowing money from family or friends?

Making Big Purchases: Cash or Credit

Jake: Hey, Lisa. I'm thinking about buying a new couch, but I'm stuck between paying **in cash** or putting it on my credit card. What do you think?

Lisa: Well, Jake, it depends. Have you **saved up** enough to pay **upfront**, or would using your credit card help you **spread out** the cost over a few months?

Jake: I have some money saved, but I'd have to **dip into** my emergency fund to pay cash. That makes me a little nervous.

Lisa: Yeah, I hear you. You don't want to **drain** your savings just for a couch. But if you put it on your credit card, can you **keep up with** the payments? Interest can **add up** fast if you're not careful.

Jake: That's what worries me. I've been trying to **pay off** some of my other balances, so adding more debt feels like a step backward.

Lisa: Maybe you could look for a store that offers **zero-interest financing**. That way, you can **break down** the payments without paying extra.

Jake: That's a good idea. I'll check if the furniture store has that option. But don't you think cash gives you more bargaining power?

Lisa: Absolutely! When you're paying **on the spot**, some places might be willing to **knock off** a few bucks. It doesn't hurt to ask.

Jake: True, but I hate the idea of completely wiping out my emergency fund. What do you usually do for big purchases?

Lisa: I try to **weigh the pros and cons**. If it's something I can't wait for, like a fridge that's on its last legs, I'll use a credit card. Otherwise, I'd rather wait and **save up** so I don't have to worry about monthly payments.

Jake: Makes sense. I'll shop around and see if I can find a deal with financing. Worst case, I'll use some cash and leave the rest for emergencies.

Lisa: That sounds like a solid plan. Just make sure you don't **overspend**. It's easy to get carried away when you're buying furniture.

Jake: Thanks for the advice, Lisa. I'll **think it through** and make the best choice for my situation.

Glossary:

In cash: Paying with physical money instead of a card.
Saved up: To accumulate money over time for a specific purpose.
Upfront: Paying the full amount at the time of purchase.
Spread out: To divide into smaller parts over a period of time.
Dip into: To use part of something, usually money or resources.
Drain: To use up completely.
Keep up with: To maintain regular payments or progress.
Add up: To increase gradually over time.
Pay off: To completely settle a debt or balance.
Break down: To divide into smaller, manageable parts.
On the spot: Immediately and without delay.
Knock off: To reduce the price of something.
Weigh the pros and cons: To consider the advantages and disadvantages.
Save up: To gather money for a specific goal.
Overspend: To spend more money than you planned or can afford.
Think it through: To carefully consider all aspects of a decision.

Speaking time

What are the advantages and disadvantages of using cash versus credit for big purchases?
Have you ever regretted a big purchase? What would you do differently next time?

The Pros and Cons of Payday Loans

Emily: Hey, Tom. I heard you're thinking about taking out a payday loan. Are you sure that's a good idea?

Tom: Yeah, I'm short on cash this month, and I need to **cover** my car repair bill. It's the only way I can **get by** until my next paycheck.

Emily: I get that, but payday loans can really **catch up with you**. The interest rates are crazy high.

Tom: I know they're not ideal, but I don't have many options right now. My credit card is maxed out, and I don't want to **ask for** money from friends or family.

Emily: Still, those loans can **pile up** quickly. Did you check the terms? They often charge fees that can **add up** before you know it.

Tom: Yeah, I read the fine print. The plan is to pay it off as soon as I can so I don't **rack up** too much interest.

Emily: That's a smart move, but what if something else **comes up**? If you can't pay it off on time, it could really **set you back** financially.

Tom: That's true. I'm trying to **think it through**, but I feel stuck. Have you ever had to take out a payday loan?

Emily: I almost did once, but I ended up **reaching out** to my bank instead. They offered me a small personal loan with a much lower interest rate. Maybe you could check with them?

Tom: I didn't think about that. I guess it's worth a shot. It'd be nice to **get out of** this financial mess without digging a deeper hole.

Emily: Exactly. Payday loans might seem like a quick fix, but they can be a slippery slope. If you can, try to **hold off** and explore other options first.

Tom: Thanks, Emily. I'll check with my bank and see if they can help me **sort this out**. You've given me a lot to think about.

Emily: Anytime, Tom. Just don't let those payday lenders **take advantage of you**. You've got other ways to figure this out.

Glossary:

Cover: To pay for something or make up a financial shortfall.
Get by: To manage with what you have, especially financially.
Catch up with you: To have negative consequences that accumulate over time.
Ask for: To request help, money, or favors.
Pile up: To accumulate in a way that becomes overwhelming.
Add up: To increase in amount over time.
Rack up: To accumulate a large amount, often debt or points.
Comes up: To happen unexpectedly.
Set you back: To delay or hinder progress, often financially.
Think it through: To carefully consider all aspects of a decision.
Reaching out: To contact someone for help or support.
Get out of: To escape or avoid a difficult situation.
Hold off: To delay or postpone doing something.
Sort this out: To resolve or fix a problem.
Take advantage of: To exploit someone, often in an unfair way.

Speaking time

What are some alternatives to payday loans that people could consider?

Have you ever been in a financial situation where you needed quick cash? How did you handle it?

Sharing Expenses with Roommates

Mia: Hey, Jake, do you have a minute? I think we need to **go over** our monthly expenses again.
Jake: Sure, Mia. What's up? Is something **off** with the bills?
Mia: Kind of. I noticed we're not splitting things evenly. I've been **chipping in** a little extra for the electricity bill, and it's starting to **add up**.

Jake: Oh man, I didn't realize that. I thought we were all **keeping track of** what we owe.

Mia: Yeah, but sometimes the smaller stuff, like cleaning supplies or Wi-Fi, **slips through the cracks**. It's not a big deal, but I think we need to **sort it out**.

Jake: Totally fair. Should we **set up** some kind of spreadsheet to **keep tabs on** everything? That way, we can all **pitch in** the right amounts.

Mia: That's a good idea. We could also **chip away at** any past differences. For example, I know I still owe you for the groceries last week.

Jake: Oh yeah, I forgot about that. No worries, though—it all **evens out** eventually. But yeah, a spreadsheet would help us **stay on top of** things.

Mia: Exactly. And maybe we should also **lay down some ground rules** for shared stuff. Like, if one of us buys something for the apartment, we **split the cost** right away instead of waiting.

Jake: Agreed. Let's also **figure out** a better way to handle unexpected expenses, like repairs or upgrades.

Mia: For sure. Maybe we can **put aside** a little money each month for that stuff.

Jake: Great idea. I'll **get started on** the spreadsheet, and we can go through it together later.

Mia: Sounds like a plan. Thanks for being open about this, Jake. I didn't want it to **turn into** a bigger issue.

Jake: No problem, Mia. Communication's key when you're sharing a place. Let's make this work!

Glossary:
Go over: To review or discuss something in detail.
Off: Not correct or accurate.
Chipping in: Contributing money or effort toward something.
Add up: To accumulate over time.
Keeping track of: Monitoring or staying aware of something.
Slips through the cracks: To be forgotten or overlooked.
Sort it out: To resolve or clarify an issue.
Set up: To establish or create something.
Keep tabs on: To monitor or keep an eye on something.
Pitch in: To contribute or help with something.
Chip away at: To gradually reduce or fix something.
Evens out: To balance or become fair over time.
Stay on top of: To remain in control or up to date with something.
Lay down some ground rules: To establish rules or guidelines.
Split the cost: To divide expenses equally.
Figure out: To understand or come to a solution.
Put aside: To save money for a specific purpose.

Get started on: To begin working on something.
Turn into: To develop into something else, often more serious.

Speaking time
What are some strategies for sharing expenses fairly with roommates?
Have you ever had a disagreement about shared costs? How did you handle it?

Charitable Giving on a Budget

Emma: Hey, Liam, have you ever thought about giving to charity?
Liam: Yeah, I've **thought it over** a few times, but money's been tight lately. It's hard to **set aside** extra cash when you're on a budget.
Emma: I totally get it. But I've found ways to **chip in** without breaking the bank.

Liam: Really? How do you manage that?
Emma: For starters, I **cut back on** little things, like grabbing coffee every day. That money can really **add up** over time.
Liam: That's smart. So, do you just **hand over** the money to a charity?
Emma: Sometimes, but I also like to **look into** local organizations. That way, I know exactly where my money's going.
Liam: Makes sense. Have you ever thought about donating your time instead?
Emma: Absolutely! Volunteering is a great way to **give back** without spending a dime.
Liam: I've been meaning to **check out** that food bank downtown. Maybe I could start there.
Emma: That's a great idea. And if you're donating money, some charities even let you **set up** small recurring donations. Even $5 a month can **make a difference**.
Liam: I like that. It's easier to **keep up with** small amounts than to give a big chunk all at once.
Emma: Exactly. And don't forget about things like donating clothes or household items. It's a great way to **clear out** your space and help someone in need.
Liam: True. I have some stuff I've been meaning to **get rid of**. I should **round it up** and drop it off.
Emma: There you go! Every little bit counts. It's not about how much you give—it's about showing you care.

Liam: Thanks, Emma. You've really **opened my eyes** to some practical ways to give back.
Emma: Anytime, Liam. Let me know if you want to volunteer together sometime!

Glossary:
Thought it over: Considered something carefully.
Set aside: Save or reserve something, usually money or time.
Chip in: Contribute money or effort.
Cut back on: Reduce spending or use of something.
Add up: Accumulate over time.
Hand over: Give something directly to someone.
Look into: Investigate or research something.
Give back: Contribute to the community or help others.
Check out: Explore or investigate something.
Set up: Arrange or establish something.
Make a difference: Have a positive impact.
Keep up with: Maintain or stay consistent with something.
Clear out: Remove unnecessary items from a space.
Get rid of: Eliminate or dispose of something.
Round it up: Gather or collect items together.
Opened my eyes: Made someone aware of something they didn't realize before.

Speaking time
What are some creative ways to contribute to charity without spending much money?

How do you decide which charities or causes to support?

Money Habits in Different Cultures

Alex: Hey, Mia, have you ever noticed how different cultures handle money?

Mia: Oh, for sure. It's fascinating! Some cultures really **hold on to** traditional ways of saving, while others are more into spending.

Alex: Exactly. When I traveled to Japan, I saw how much they focus on saving and avoiding debt. They're really careful not to **rack up** credit card balances.

Mia: That's so smart. I think in the U.S., people tend to **live it up** and spend on things they might not need.

Alex: True, but I've heard that in Italy, people **shell out** on food and family gatherings because those are such big parts of their lives.

Mia: That makes sense. In some cultures, like India, there's a strong habit of **setting aside** money for family events, like weddings. It's almost like an unspoken rule.

Alex: Yeah, and in Scandinavian countries, they focus on **keeping track of** expenses and investing in experiences rather than stuff.

Mia: I love that. It's a great way to **make the most of** your money. Have you noticed how some cultures prefer cash over credit?

Alex: Oh, totally. When I went to Germany, they really **stick to** cash. It's like they don't trust credit cards as much.

Mia: That's so interesting. In contrast, Americans often **rely on** credit cards for points and rewards.

Alex: Yep, but that can also lead to trouble if you don't **pay off** your balance each month.

Mia: No kidding. It's all about balance. I think we can all **pick up** good habits from different cultures, though.

Alex: For sure. Like learning to **cut back on** unnecessary spending or being more thoughtful about big purchases.
Mia: Agreed. It's cool how money habits reflect cultural values. It's not just about numbers; it's about what people prioritize.
Alex: Totally. So, what's one habit you'd like to **take on** from another culture?
Mia: Hmm, I'd love to **get into** the habit of tracking expenses better, like they do in Scandinavian countries. What about you?
Alex: I think I'd focus on **saving up** for experiences, like trips or events. It feels more meaningful than just buying things.
Mia: That's a great idea. Let's start doing that!

Glossary:
Hold on to: Keep something or not let it go.
Rack up: Accumulate, usually debts or points.
Live it up: Enjoy life extravagantly.
Shell out: Spend money on something.
Set aside: Save or reserve money or time.
Keeping track of: Monitoring or recording something.
Make the most of: Use something in the best way possible.
Stick to: Follow something strictly.
Rely on: Depend on something or someone.
Pay off: Settle a debt in full.
Pick up: Learn or adopt something new.
Cut back on: Reduce the amount of something.
Take on: Start doing or adopting something.
Get into: Develop an interest or habit.

Saving up: Accumulating money for a specific purpose.

Speaking time
What money habits from other cultures would you like to adopt and why?
How do money habits in your culture reflect its values?

About the author

Evert González is a seasoned English teacher and accomplished writer, recognized for his expertise in language education and literary prowess. With a passion for fostering language proficiency, Evert has not only excelled in the classroom but has also made a significant mark in the literary world. His portfolio boasts a collection of books spanning both English and Spanish, showcasing his versatile command over languages. As an author, Evert combines his linguistic acumen with a creative flair, crafting engaging narratives that resonate with readers of diverse backgrounds. Through his works, Evert González continues to inspire language learners and literature enthusiasts alike, leaving an indelible impact on the realms of education and storytelling. Evert González is a seasoned English teacher and accomplished writer, recognized for his expertise in language education and literary prowess. With a passion for fostering language proficiency, Evert has not only excelled in the classroom but has also made a significant mark in the literary world. His portfolio boasts a collection of books spanning both English and Spanish, showcasing his versatile command over languages. As an author, Evert combines his linguistic acumen with a creative flair, crafting engaging narratives that resonate with readers of diverse backgrounds. Through his works, Evert González continues to inspire language learners and literature enthusiasts alike, leaving an indelible impact on the realms of education and storytelling.

Conclusion

In the concluding section of "Wacky Money," readers embark on a final journey that not only ties together the linguistic threads woven throughout the book but also serves as a springboard for ongoing language exploration.

Recap of Key Vocabulary and Phrasal Verbs: This section serves as a valuable resource for readers, offering a concise recapitulation of the key vocabulary and phrasal verbs encountered in each chapter. Through a systematic review, learners can reinforce their understanding of essential financial language, ensuring a solid foundation for future linguistic endeavors.

Encouragement for Continued Learning:

The conclusion is not a farewell but a call to action. Readers are encouraged to view the mastery of financial English as an ongoing pursuit. Whether engaging in further reading, participating in language exchanges, or incorporating financial discussions into daily life, the encouragement provided aims to inspire learners to persist on their language learning journey.

The encouragement extends beyond the book, fostering a mindset that embraces challenges and celebrates victories in the continuous evolution of language proficiency. A reminder that language learning is a dynamic, lifelong process, and every step taken contributes to an enriched linguistic repertoire.

Acknowledgments and Resources

This section pays homage to the collaborative efforts that brought "Wacky Money" to fruition. Acknowledgments express gratitude to individuals, educators, and resources that contributed to the creation of the book. It serves as a moment of appreciation for the collective endeavor that enhances the learning experience.

Additionally, a curated list of resources is provided to guide readers in their further exploration of both language learning and financial topics. From recommended reading materials to online language platforms, this section equips readers with tools to expand their knowledge and proficiency independently.

In essence, the conclusion is not the end but a transition—a bridge from the structured learning environment of the book to the vast landscape of real-world language use. It encourages readers to carry the knowledge gained and the skills honed into their everyday interactions, fostering a language-rich and financially savvy communication style.

As readers close the final chapter of "Mastering Money Matters," they do so not as passive participants but as empowered communicators ready to navigate the complex language of finance with finesse and confidence. The conclusion serves as a catalyst for the next phase of their linguistic journey—one that is dynamic, rewarding, and filled with endless possibilities.

www.ingramcontent.com/pod-product-compliance
Lightning Source LLC
Chambersburg PA
CBHW050050230526
45470CB00004B/1477